Preschool and Your Child

Preschool and Your Child

What You Should Know

Diana Townsend-Butterworth

WALKER AND COMPANY
NEW YORK

First published in the United States of America in 1995 by Walker
Publishing Company, Inc.

Published simultaneously in Canada by Thomas Allen & Son Canada,
Limited, Markham, Ontario

Library of Congress Cataloging-in-Publication Data
Townsend-Butterworth, Diana.
Preschool and your child : what you should know / Diana Townsend-
Butterworth.
p.   cm.
Selected from : Your child's first school. 1992.
Includes bibliographical references and index.
ISBN 0-8027-7472-5 (pbk.)
1. Nursery schools—United States.   2. Education, Preschool—
United States.   I. Townsend-Butterworth, Diana.   Your child's
first school.   II. Title.
LB1140.23.T69   1995
372.21'0973—dc20   95-23002
CIP

Printed in the United States of America

2   4   6   8   10   9   7   5   3   1

Contents

•• •• •• ••

Preface

What do we need to know about our children and preschool? Unlike our VCRs, fax machines, CD players, and dishwashers, our children don't come with instruction manuals or guarantees, and so we turn to books to give us advice and confidence.

Before my son was born my apartment was piled high with books—on pregnancy, childbirth, and then later on breast feeding and child development. The books were very helpful. Everything went along just as they promised, until one day when my son, James, was about eighteen months old. We were in the playground in the park, and suddenly the mother of a three-year-old who was building castles in the sandbox with James, turned to me and said, "Where is your son going to go to preschool?"

I looked at her in disbelief. I didn't even know whether I wanted James to go to preschool. I didn't know when he would be ready and, more important, I didn't know when I would be ready for him to be ready. So off I went to the bookstore to look for a book that would tell me when, where, and how, and even whether my son should go to preschool. And for the first time I couldn't find a book to answer my questions. I tried the library. No luck. I was on my own. And so I began my own research on the where, when, and how of preschool. When I had found the answers to all my questions and my son was happily ensconced in an appropriate preschool, I started thinking about the other six million parents out there facing similar decisions about preschool. I realized that most parents don't have the time or resources to do their own research. I decided to share my findings with parents all across this country—parents who care deeply about their child's first school experience. And so the idea for this book was born.

As I wrote, I drew on my own past experience as an academic researcher, as a teacher, and as the head of a junior school, as well as on my current experience as the parent of a child in preschool. I interviewed educators, pediatricians, and child psychologists. I reviewed the research in academic journals. I visited preschools all across the country. I talked to parents and watched children learning how to explore their world and make friends.

What should you know about your child and preschool?

You need to know

•• WHAT preschool is all about and what you should and shouldn't expect it to do for your child.
•• WHY your child should or shouldn't go to preschool. And what the alternatives are if you want to keep your child at home.
•• WHEN your child will be ready and when you will be ready for your child to be ready.
•• WHERE to send your child to preschool—what the differences are in preschools, and how to explore your options.
•• HOW to choose a school where your child will flourish and where you can be an involved, supportive parent.

You also need to know that no matter where you live or how much money you have, you have a choice in the quality of your child's education. You need to know how to exercise that choice, and you need to know how to find an effective preschool with an age appropriate curriculum. You need to know your own goals and expectations. And last but not least you need to understand the needs of your own child.

This book is written for you—the parents of young children. It is about the choices we make as parents. It is about finding preschools for our children that will nourish them and help them grow up feeling confident and successful. It is about knowing how to help our children develop in their own way, at their own pace, as we launch them on a lifelong voyage of learning and discovery.

Preschool and Your Child

ONE

The Basic Ingredients of a Good Early Childhood Program or School

A good early childhood program teaches social skills, how to share toys and play together. It stresses physical coordination and develops motor skills . . . it introduces youngsters to the joys of learning . . . an appetite that, once created, carries over into the school years.

—FROM THE NATIONAL
ASSOCIATION OF ELEMENTARY
SCHOOL PRINCIPALS' "REPORT
TO PARENTS"

Good early childhood programs or schools are based on the development of the whole child. They provide a safe, nurturing environment that fosters the emotional, social, and cognitive development of children. Good schools and programs recognize that play is fundamental to the intellectual development of young children. According to Ellen Galinsky, codirector of the Families and Work Institute in New York City, "The preschooler learns through direct experience by doing and acting upon his environment. In touching, tasting, seeking, hearing, experimenting, and playing, the child builds ideas and concepts."[1] As Pam Loree, who has taught young children for nearly twenty years, first in a lab school at Kansas State University, then in Texas, and now at St. Bernard's School in New York City, said to me, "It is attitude, not the acquisition of skills, that is the crucial ingredient of early childhood school. A child who is drilled for certain tasks before he or she is ready won't end up being any smarter. Doing it sooner doesn't necessarily make it any better in the long run and it can be damaging to a child's self-esteem."

It is important for young children to develop a positive attitude

•• •• •• ••

about themselves. Countless teachers have told me that they have found over the years that when the children in their classrooms lack a positive sense of self or when they can't get along with others, they are seldom able to learn at an optimal level regardless of how many sight words they can identify or esoteric facts they can memorize. If children are always worrying about whether or not they are really okay or about what their peers think of them, their ability to learn will be affected no matter how intelligent they are.

Good early childhood schools and programs help children develop self-esteem by giving children opportunities to learn about themselves and their world. They provide experiences that will challenge but not frustrate or overwhelm the child— experiences that will help the child develop a sense of competency, that will let a child feel successful. Good early childhood schools and programs help children learn to play together and share their toys. It is here that children begin to learn that different behaviors can be appropriate at different times and places. Children develop a willingness to listen and to pay attention, to focus in on a task and to complete it, to develop expectations, and to set and achieve goals. Children learn many things in good early childhood schools and programs, but the most important thing they learn is how to get along with others and how to function effectively in a group.

•• Early Childhood Classrooms

My research has taken me into many different early childhood classrooms in small towns and large cities around the country. In one of the classrooms I visited, a small boy with large black eyes and shaggy hair was standing at an easel. His clothes were covered with paint. There was a look of intense concentration on his face as he watched the red paint from his brush drip down the paper. In another corner of the room six children were clustered around a table covered with plastic knives, wooden spoons, mixing bowls, and an assortment of apples, bananas, tangerines, strawberries, peaches, and blueberries. The teacher told me that a note had gone home with the children the night before asking each one to bring in a piece of fruit. Now they were all busy scraping, cutting, measuring, and mixing while the teacher read directions from a recipe. The children were making fruit salad for morning snack.

In a classroom in a different city, a boy in a chef's hat is standing in front of a toy stove pouring imaginary ingredients into pots and stirring them up. Across the room two children are sitting at a table fitting together pieces of a puzzle. A small blonde girl with pigtails, red high-heeled shoes, blue beads, and a briefcase toddles purposefully toward a toy telephone. She tells me she is on her way to work but she has to call home first. Meanwhile in the block corner, a boy and a girl have just finished building a spaceship out of hardwood blocks. The boy is filling the spaceship with plastic astronauts. The girl is dictating the words she wants the teacher to put on a sign: "Jennifer's and Michael's Spaceship. Please Do Not Touch!"

In a third classroom in yet another school, I see a group of children sitting on the floor in a circle. A teacher is playing a guitar. The children sing as they help five spiders climb up the waterspout with vigorous hand and body movements. Meanwhile, a boy is sitting on a chair in the house corner in front of a row of dolls. He has a book in his hand from the reading corner. He explains to me that he is a teacher reading to his class. He reads in a loud clear voice with lots of expression. I notice that he is holding the book upside down.

In another classroom in another town I watch a group of children work on a class mural on sea life. The teacher tells me that the previous day the class had gone on a trip to the aquarium and now the children are making pictures of what they saw. One child is busy cutting up small pieces of brightly colored paper. Another is gluing the pieces onto a large sheet of paper attached to the wall. A third is gluing on a design of dried-up macaroni, and a fourth is covering all the glued-on pieces with sprinkles. Next to the mural is a large piece of paper with the name of each child written in large bold letters. Beside the names the teacher has written what each child liked best about the aquarium.

Each of the early childhood classrooms I visited had a wide variety of interesting materials available for the children. In all of the classrooms except the pure Montessori ones, I saw a block corner filled with hardwood blocks of different sizes and shapes, a housekeeping area with a stove and cabinets and pots and pans, a dress-up area, a sand table and/or a water table, a carpentry bench, and a story corner with lots of big pillows and picture books. I saw easels and paints and markers and clay and other art supplies. In many classrooms there was a nature area where the children had planted different kinds of seeds and were watching them grow. There were gerbils and guinea pigs and turtles or other small animals. One of the classrooms I visited had a lop-eared rabbit called Miss Tulip hopping around, and another had a snake called Samson that was being held affectionately by a little girl named Sara. There were neatly labeled bins of small plastic figures and cars and trucks and puzzles and games and beads and pegboards. There were outdoor play areas with climbing equipment and large building blocks. With the exception of Montessori classrooms, where specially developed materials are structured to be used in a specific way and in a designated sequence, most early childhood materials are "open-ended," which means that there is no one right way to play with them. Children are free, in fact encouraged, to explore these materials and invent new ways to use them.

I did not see a work sheet or a flash card on any of my classroom visits. I did not see children memorizing number facts or studying spelling words or puzzling over words in readers. Yet the children were quite clearly learning many things, including mathematical concepts and communication skills and even word recognition. These children, like the children in many of the other good early childhood schools I visited, were all happily involved in age-appropriate activities. They were also all participating in carefully planned early childhood programs. To the uninitiated eye everything in one of these classrooms may appear to be happening by chance, but the teachers have all structured their rooms and planned their programs to motivate children to use the materials they have provided in a positive way. Each teacher knows exactly which concepts and skills are being learned in each of the classrooms I described. As the year progresses the materials will change and the experiences will expand as the children develop new interests and capabilities.

Parents and other adults who have never been trained in early childhood education are apt to see all curricula in terms of reading, writing, and arithmetic. But the early childhood teacher has a curriculum, too, and it isn't focused primarily on the traditional three R's. Curriculum for the early childhood teacher is the planning and structuring of age-appropriate experiences that will motivate students to learn important skills and concepts. But even more importantly it is the encouragement of creativity and intellectual curiosity.

•• Understanding Terminology

Early childhood educational programs are known by a confusing variety of names. Sometimes we call them *schools*, and sometimes we refer to them as *centers* or *programs*. Early childhood school, preschool, nursery school, kindergarten, pre-K, infant school, preprimary, first program, learning center, toddler program, Head Start, extended day, and daycare are all names you may encounter. To confuse things further, the names themselves may have different meanings in different parts of the country. Some regions use the term *daycare* to refer to any program for six or more children under the age of six regardless of whether the program is educational or custodial. Other regions prefer to use the terms *preschool, pre-K,* or *nursery school* to distinguish programs with educational goals. *Nursery school* is frequently used to refer to private schools with half-day programs for three-, four-, and five-year-olds. *Daycare,* on the other hand, has traditionally meant full-day programs designed to care for children while their parents are at work. However, many nursery schools are now offering full-day and even extended-day programs. Parents who use daycare facilities are in turn demanding quality care for their children that will foster their physical, social, emotional, and intellectual development. Distinctions between nursery school and daycare are blurring as each evolves into more comprehensive groups of services for children and their families.

Despite the efforts of the National Association for the Education of Young Children (NAEYC) and the National Association of Nursery School Directors to define the field of early childhood education and to convince people to use a common set of terms, the confusion persists. Instead of adopting the NAEYC's preferred term "early childhood school," parents and teachers are still using a variety of different terms to describe a child's first school experience. In an attempt to avoid further confusion, I have elected to use the term *early childhood school* to describe educational programs for children under the age of six that take place outside the home in semiformalized group settings.

·· Types of Early Childhood Schools

When you start to investigate early childhood schools for your children, you will again hear many different names used to describe the various types of schools. Some of the names you will hear are Montessori, progressive, developmental-interaction, traditional, academic, structured, unstructured, open, closed, formal, informal, whole child, total child, child-centered, Waldorf, direct instruction, cognitive, eclectic, all-day. Whatever term a school uses to define its program, it is important for you to find out what that particular school means by the term because, as I noted earlier, there is no consensus on the meaning of specific terms used to describe early childhood schools. One school that calls itself "progressive" may in fact be very different from another school that uses a similar term to describe its program and philosophy. With that word of caution in mind, we will look at some of the approaches to early childhood education generally associated with the more frequently used terms.

·· MONTESSORI SCHOOLS ··

Schools that operate in a pure Montessori tradition use the materials developed by Maria Montessori in a special way and in a specially planned sequence. The main interaction is between the child and the materials, not between the child and other children or between the child and the teacher. Montessori believed that the teacher's role is to guide children to appropriate materials and demonstrate their correct use. The emphasis is on self-directed learning, and because children of similar ages may be working at different levels, Montessori saw no need to group them by chronological age. Most Montessori classrooms have children from ages three to six working side by side. Montessori believed that children must learn to deal with reality before confronting fantasy. Montessori stories are based on fact, and there is no place for dress-up or pretend play in a pure Montessori classroom. Many Montessori schools in this country, particularly those that belong to the American Montessori Society as opposed to the Association Montessori Internationale, do not adhere strictly to all the original Montessori principles, and instead draw some of their ideas from other traditions. In these schools you may find children using open-ended materials such as blocks and clay as well as the special Montessori materials. You will also see children involved in dramatic or fantasy play.

••WALDORF OR RUDOLF STEINER SCHOOLS••

In a Waldorf school the teacher is the key in the learning process. Rudolf Steiner, who started the first Waldorf school in Germany shortly after the end of World War I, believed that young children learn by imitating the behavior and words of those around them. Here, the teacher is both an authority figure and a source of important information. The children's love and respect for their teacher is seen as the primary motivation toward learning. Steiner believed that children must first gain a sense of their own bodies through play and a variety of physical activities and hands-on experience with various art forms before they can begin to develop their intellects. Steiner also believed that young children experience the world through pictures and movement. Hence painting, modeling with clay, crafts, music, dance, and drama are emphasized, and no academics are taught before the age of six or seven.

••PROGRESSIVE SCHOOLS••

A progressive school is one that is based on the philosophy developed by John Dewey in the early part of this century. It is often referred to as the "whole child" or "total child" or "child-centered" approach. Play is seen as the child's work. It is the medium through which learning takes place and children come to understand their environment. Open-ended materials such as blocks, sand, water, clay, and paint are emphasized, and children are encouraged to engage in dramatic play.

However, the most important interaction in a progressive classroom is between children working together in groups rather than between an individual child and a specific educational material. In the 1950s Dewey's ideas fell into disrepute as many people erroneously interpreted them as advocating permissiveness and aimless, undirected play. Today many educators are taking a new look at Dewey's ideas as they increasingly realize the importance of children's physical, emotional, social, and psychological needs, as well as their intellectual needs. The late Lawrence A. Cremin, former president of Teachers College at Columbia University, has said, "The return to Dewey . . . may be partly a response to the fundamental changes that education and society are facing, changes similar to Dewey's era. . . . The difficulties of educating everyone are being recognized and confronted, making the solutions Dewey proposed relevant once again."[2] Many schools that do not refer to themselves as "progressive" use the open-ended materials and many of the methods developed by Dewey and other progressive educators.

••DEVELOPMENTAL-INTERACTION, OR THE BANK STREET MODEL SCHOOL••

One of the offshoots of the progressive tradition is the developmental-interaction approach developed at the Bank Street College of Education in New York. *Developmental* refers to the growth and development of children and the increasing complexity of the ways they respond to experiences, then organize and process their responses. *Interaction* refers to children's interaction with their immediate environment. Development is seen not as something that just happens to a child but instead as a direct result of a child's interaction with his or her environment. As Harriet Cuffaro, a member of the Bank Street faculty, says, development comes from "the child's doing, making, questioning, testing, trying, formulating, experiencing."[3] "Individuality," "socialization," "competence," and "integration" are words frequently used to describe the process by which children gradually learn how to use various skills, to make choices, to take responsibility for their actions, and to synthesize and understand their experiences. The key interaction is between children rather than between an individual child and materials. The teacher is also a central figure who creates the appropriate environment to foster learning. The core of the curriculum revolves around social studies, which is seen as an interdisciplinary study of our world and the different issues we confront. The emphasis, in line with the Dewey philosophy, is on solving real-life problems. Concepts are taught through the use of concrete, open-ended materials, as an integral part of the entire program rather than as separate entities. The atmosphere is usually informal and teachers may be called by their first names.

••TRADITIONAL OR STRUCTURED SCHOOLS••

Schools referred to as "traditional" or "structured" are usually based on varying interpretations of Piaget's cognitive theories as well as the developmental stages of Gesell. They are sometimes also called "academic," "cognitive," or "formal." The use of the word "traditional" to describe these schools is in fact somewhat of a contradiction in terms, since "traditional" originally referred to nursery schools in which there was little focus on a child's cognitive development. The schools we refer to today as "traditional" or "structured" are concerned, just as the progressive and developmental-interaction schools are, with the whole child—with physical, social, emotional, and cognitive development. These schools have the same kinds of open-ended materials found in developmental-interaction and progressive schools. They may even use some Montessori materials as well. The rooms in fact often look very similar to developmental-interaction and progressive classrooms. The atmosphere, while still warm and friendly, may seem a bit more formal, and teachers are seldom called by their first names.

The main difference, however lies in the role of the teacher, who tends to be more directive. She or he usually sets clear limits and has quite specific expectations and goals. There are well-defined lists of developmentally appropriate skills to be mastered, such as sorting and patterning, sequencing, listening, following directions, remembering details, and expressing ideas verbally. The children learn the skills through the manipulation of concrete materials, in dramatic play, and by interacting with their environment. However, activities such as finger painting and tracing shapes in the sand are seen by the teachers as reading-readiness activities. Teachers actively encourage children to think and talk about the things they are doing. Children are usually taught letters and sounds as well as shapes and colors. Sometimes schools have a letter or color of the week. If it is *J* week, for instance, children might learn about jaguars, jump rope at recess, make jam, and have jelly beans for snacks. A few traditional schools use work sheets to reinforce concepts.

Some traditional schools use specially developed curricula based on different educators' interpretations of Piaget's theories. One of these curricula was developed by Celia Lavatelli, who believed that while some children make exciting discoveries on their own, others benefit from a more structured approach and need additional direction to develop problem-solving skills and to learn to think logically. In the Lavatelli curriculum, specific cognitive tasks such as sequencing, measuring, and classifying are taught in short ten- to fifteen-minute training sessions. Children may be asked to make a necklace out of beads following a particular pattern demonstrated by the teacher. Teachers are trained to comment on the children's work, to ask questions, and to encourage children to discuss and actively think about what they are doing and why.

Another curriculum based on Piaget's work, the High/Scope Curriculum, is a cognitively oriented curriculum developed by David Weikart, president of High/Scope Educational Research Foundation in Ypsilanti, Michigan. Here again teachers actively intervene and structure children's play to develop cognitive skills. The day usually begins with all the children getting together while the teacher reviews a list of available activities and the children choose among them. After the children have worked on their various activities, they meet again to discuss what they have done, the progress they have made, and any problems they may have encountered. Later there is an outdoor playtime for large–motor skill development—running, hopping, and climbing—and a circle time for more discussion, storytelling, and singing.

Many good traditional schools do not use any one specific curriculum but are really rather eclectic in nature. They have a middle-of-the-road philosophy using what one early childhood teacher referred to as "the tried and true of many different approaches." Rather than adhering to a single specific curriculum, these schools combine what they consider to be the most successful elements of a variety of different early childhood traditions.

••Direct Instruction, or Academic Schools••

In the direct-instruction approach most activities are initiated by the teacher, and the children's role is to give the required response at the appropriate time. Direct instruction is loosely based on some of the programmed learning theories of the late behavioral psychologist B. F. Skinner. Stimuli, response, and positive reinforcement are all key components of Skinner's theories. DISTAR, one of the curricula sometimes used in direct instruction, was originally developed by Carl Bereiter and Siegfried Engelmann for use in Follow Through, an intervention program for economically disadvantaged children. DISTAR provides children with up to an hour and a half of direct instruction each day. Children are taught to read phonetically—first learning sounds through constant repetition, then putting the sounds together to form words. They are also drilled on simple number facts and taught to count by rote. This whole approach is highly controversial. Douglas Carnine, a professor of education at the University of Oregon, has said, "Some kids, particularly disadvantaged kids, may come from unstimulating homes—they may never be ready. If they don't get an academic orientation in kindergarten, they may never grow into successful students."[4] Other educators such as David Elkind, a psychologist at Tufts University and author of many books on the education of young children, feel that highly structured direct teaching approaches can cause children to become rote learners, inhibiting their natural curiosity and desire to learn and hampering their sense of initiative and independent problem-solving abilities.

•• Making a Comparison

A number of research studies have sought to compare different types of early childhood schools and their effects on children in elementary school and beyond. Proponents of the Montessori method believe it encourages children to work at their own pace and build on their own knowledge. On the other hand, a recent study by Rheta DeVries, director of the Human Development Laboratory School at the University of Houston, found that "Montessori preschool children scored substantially lower than children from a more group-oriented preschool program on tests of social skills."[5] A 1984 study conducted by the late Louise Miller at the University of Louisville found that by tenth grade male students who had gone to Montessori preschools scored higher on tests of creative thinking and academic achievement but female students scored lower.[6] Many of the studies, beginning with the Perry Preschool Study and the High/Scope Preschool Curriculum Study, have looked at children from economically disadvantaged backgrounds. It is not known whether the conclusions drawn from these studies apply to children from middle-class backgrounds.

A variety of studies show that children who have attended traditional or structured early childhood schools are generally more task-oriented and less aggressive with their peers. They also tend to do better on achievement and IQ tests. On the negative side, they show less independence and initiative, and their play is apt to be less imaginative. Children who have attended progressive or unstructured schools are usually seen as more independent and more apt to ask questions. They usually score higher on tests of problem solving and curiosity but lower on achievement and IQ tests.

Most early childhood schools in reality fall somewhere in between the extremes of structured and unstructured. Many combine some teacher-directed activities with ample opportunities for free play and interaction with peers. After reviewing relevant studies, Alison Clarke-Stewart, professor at the University of California at Irvine, has concluded in her book *Daycare* that the evidence points to "the benefits—for constructive activity, for intelligence, for later achievement, for positive motivation, persistence, and problem solving, and for social skills—of a preschool program that blends prescribed educational activities with opportunities for free choice, that has some structure, but also allows children to explore a rich environment of objects and peers on their own without teacher direction."[7] My own experience leads me to agree with her conclusion.

•• Goals of Early Childhood Schools

Sometimes you will find a school's goals explicitly stated in catalogs and other written material, but often you will have to ferret goals out for yourself by talking to the director and asking some probing questions. Good early childhood schools do not all look and feel exactly alike. Even among the same general types of schools, the atmosphere and the specific materials vary according to the individual personalities and philosophies of the teachers and directors. Some schools may put more emphasis on teaching children how to work together in a group, while others encourage children to spend the greater part of their day exploring materials independently. However, there are certain goals that many good early childhood schools do have in common. Based on my conversations with early childhood teachers and directors, on a careful study of the goals and criteria recommended by the National Association for the Education of Young Children,[8] and on my own observations in many different early childhood classrooms, I have come to the conclusion that a number of goals are shared by most good early childhood schools.

- • To promote the optimum physical, social, emotional, and intellectual growth of each child.
- • To provide an environment that is safe, warm, and nurturing, as well as stimulating.
- • To give children ready access to caring, intelligent adults throughout the day.
- • To furnish children with a variety of physical activities to enhance their physical skills and overall development.
- • To develop in each child a feeling of confidence and self-esteem.
- • To promote initiative and independence.
- • To help children learn respect for themselves and for others.
- • To stimulate a love of learning and a joy in the excitement of new experiences.
- • To foster children's awareness of others and to help them learn how to become part of a group, to share, and to take turns.
- • To help children develop a sense of responsibility for their own actions and for the well-being of others.
- • To encourage children's natural curiosity and interest in exploring their world.
- • To help children understand their environment.
- • To expose a child to a variety of new and interesting materials and experiences.
- • To give a child opportunities for imaginative play and for creative expression in music, art, movement, and dramatic activities.
- • To develop children's facility with language and their ability to communicate clearly and effectively both with classmates and with adults.
- • To expose children to a wide variety of children's literature by reading aloud and to thereby develop an ongoing interest in books and reading.
- • To help a child develop problem-solving abilities.
- • To give children a variety of experiences that will encourage the development of mathematical and scientific concepts.

13

•• To help a child develop a sense of competence through the mastery of age-appropriate physical, social, and intellectual skills using developmentally based materials and methods.
•• And last, but certainly not least, to try to create a partnership between home and school based on mutual respect and close communication.

This last goal, a sense of a partnership based on a feeling of being part of a close and caring community, is an important part of the early childhood school experience for parents and their children. Parents and children both learn from being part of an early childhood school. It is, after all, the early childhood teacher who gives parents, as well as children, their first school experience. And it is part of the responsibility of the early childhood teacher to teach parents—to teach them not only about new research in child development, about the ways young children master new skills, about how they acquire and process information, about their emotional and intellectual needs, but also something about the culture of school itself, about how to be a part of the community and to work effectively with the school for the benefit of their children.

When, how, and why our children begin school can have a profound impact on their feelings about school, on their later education, and even on their lives. We as parents must try to be sure that the decisions we make and the schools we choose are right for our children. We must choose our children's schools not because we believe certain schools will turn our three-year-olds into prodigies, but rather because we believe that the schools we choose will help our children develop their true potential over time and in ways that are developmentally appropriate. As the authors of *Changed Lives,* John R. Berrueta-Clement, David P. Weikart, and others, have written, "A person's life is not transformed in some magical way by experience in a preschool program [early childhood school]. But a successful preschool experience can permanently alter the success/failure trajectory of a person's life in significant and positive ways."[9]

There are many good early childhood schools, but no one early childhood school is right for every child. Unless you happen to live in a fairly large city, you probably won't have the option of choosing from the many different types of early childhood schools we have just looked at. There may well be only one or two schools in your neighborhood. When you do not have a lot of choice, the quality of the school is more important than its expressed philosophy. If there are no schools near you that seem to meet the criteria for good early childhood schools, you may want to consider keeping your child at home or looking into some of the alternatives to early childhood schools discussed in chapter 2 such as parent cooperatives and "mommy and me" play groups.

In this next chapter, I will point out specific things you will want to look for in an early childhood school. And we will explore together ways to tell if an early childhood school is right for you and your child.

•• •• •• ••
T W O
•• •• •• •• •• •• •• •• •• •• •• ••

A Parent's Dilemma: What to Look For, How to Choose

•• Location

Location is often the single most important factor in choosing an early childhood school. A neighborhood school is particularly important for very young children. Ideally a school should be within easy walking distance or a short car ride from home. In one mother's experience, "Being close to school makes a tremendous difference when you are trying to juggle your own schedule and get everyone out of the house in the morning. Our morning wasn't so rushed and there was time to let Ashley experiment with dressing herself and begin to develop a sense of independence. We were so close I didn't even have to worry about using a stroller. We could walk down the street together and chat with Ashley's friends and their mothers on the way to school." If there is no school within walking distance, be sure to inquire about the type of transportation required to get to the schools you are considering. Attending distant schools sometimes means a trip of various legs—perhaps two buses or a bus and a subway. This is harder on a family than just a bus or a subway by itself.

Distance may be more than just a matter of getting to and from school. It can affect after-school playdates as well. If most of the other children live in the neighborhood surrounding the school, it will not be as easy for your child to get together with those children after school. It may also be more difficult for your child and you to participate in after-school programs or play groups. It will be harder for you as a parent to spend time around the school helping out on trips or in the library. Physical

•• •• •• ••

distance from a school can increase the amount of time it takes for you to feel a part of the school and your child's life there.

If both parents in the family have a long commute to work or if you are a single working parent, you may want to consider looking at schools near your workplace rather than your home. More and more parents tell me they find it makes sense for them to send their children to a school close to their work so they can be available during the day in an emergency and also so they can spend time together on the commute in the morning and evening. The admissions director of a school in New York City reports that some parents commute happily with their children from as far away as Brooklyn, Jersey City, and Hoboken and drop their children off on the way to work in the morning.

If you have more than one child, you will probably prefer that they be in the same school. Otherwise, as one working parent of two young children said, "From the logistical point of view getting to school in the morning would be a nightmare." It is also helpful if other children in your neighborhood go to the school you choose for your child. For many parents, particularly working parents, carpooling can make a difference. It is also worth asking whether a school provides transportation. A few schools, usually those that comprise the elementary as well as the early childhood years, do provide transportation, and some private bus companies are equipped to take young children to and from school. Fees for private bus service vary greatly.

Travel and distance are relative, however. And some families seem to be able to travel comparatively long distances with little wear and tear on themselves or on their children. Other families fall apart at the mere thought of getting to a bus stop on time. The best school in the world will be unsuitable if you and your child arrive in a frantic rush and a terrible temper every morning. Before making any decisions, consider the dynamics of your own family—personalities, time, work schedules, freedom from other family obligations—to determine what makes sense for you and your child.

Remember, no rule applies to every family.

•• Educational Continuity

The next point to consider in deciding on a school is whether you want to send your child to an early childhood school or to an ongoing school (a school that goes through either elementary school or secondary school but includes an early childhood division). An ongoing school can give a sense of continuity. A three-year-old can look at an older child in the hallway and think, "This is where I'm going, this is what I'll be like some day." In some ongoing schools there is considerable interaction among the grades, and older children work with younger children either directly in the classroom or on special projects.

Parents sometimes feel a sense of relief when their child is admitted to an ongoing school, believing that their child's education is now settled and they will not have to worry about admissions again until college. However, this line of thought can backfire. When children are three or four, it is difficult, perhaps impossible, to know how they will develop and what their interests and talents will be. A school that seems perfect for a three-year-old may prove to be all wrong at thirteen. An administrator at one ongoing private school observed that over the years the bottom one-fourth of the senior class in her school had a disproportionate number of children who had entered as three-year-olds. Schools are increasingly aware of this potential problem, and in some ongoing private schools, in fact, many children are counseled out of a school they began in early childhood because they cannot keep up with the work in the higher grades. Dr. James W. Wickenden, a former dean of admissions at Princeton who was cochairman of the admissions and scholarship committee of a school that recently phased out its early childhood program, has said, "It is difficult enough to judge academic competence and strength of character with people age 17. To do that at two and a half is asking the impossible."[1] Similar problems can occur in public schools that children attend from K through 12 if a child is placed in a gifted program at the kindergarten level, and there is not sufficient flexibility to allow the child to move back and forth between it and the regular program.

On the other hand, choosing to send your child to an early childhood school gives you the opportunity to rethink the question of education a few years later, after you have observed your child in an educational setting and have more information about the way your child is developing. At that time you can consider whether you want to send your children to a public or private elementary school without having to take them out of a private school where they have already begun to make friends.

In an early childhood school, the whole focus is on early childhood. The director's mind is on blocks and climbing equipment, not physics labs and basketball courts. The teachers are trained specifically in child development and the education of young children. The physical setting is specially planned to meet the needs of small children, and all the furniture and equipment are made to scale. The atmosphere is designed to be warm and nurturing and to make small children feel at home. The youngest students can have a sense that their early childhood school is their school, designed for them the way they are now, not the way they will be some day. I have seen young children become upset when older children in an ongoing school point at them and their friends in the halls and exclaim, "Aren't they cute!" A five-year-old in early childhood school can feel the pride of being looked up to by the younger children instead of being looked down on by older children.

Given the choice between an early childhood school and an ongoing school for a three-year-old, I have a predilection toward the early childhood school. However, there are no universal right or wrong answers here—only issues to be explored in relation to your own choices and preferences. If you decide on an ongoing school, you will want to make sure that the early childhood division is considered an important and integral part of the school. If, on the other hand, you decide on an early childhood school, you will want to be sure that the ongoing schools in which you might be interested later on anticipate openings for kindergarten and first grade.

•• Half Day? Full Day? Extended Day?

Some early childhood schools have part-time programs—a few hours several days a week. Others offer full-time programs—approximately the length of a regular school day five days a week. Still others offer extended-day programs from seven-thirty in the morning until seven-thirty at night. And some schools offer parents a choice between these options. Whether you choose a half-day, a full-day, or an extended-day program will depend not only on what is available in your community but also on the nature of your child and your own schedule. Some children thrive in a full-day program, while others are exhausted after a morning or afternoon with other children and need quiet time to themselves to relax and replenish their energy. If you are working full-time, you will need to take your child's energy level and personality into consideration as you decide between either a full or extended day at school, and a combination of school and home-based child care.

•• Teachers

Teachers are the key ingredients of a good early childhood school. Good teachers come in many different styles and person-alities, but they all should be interested in young children and should clearly enjoy being with them. Early childhood teachers need to be perceptive and patient as well as intelligent. They need to be loving and warm, but they also must be able to set clear limits and be willing to enforce them. They should be trained in early childhood education. Head teachers should have a degree in early childhood education, and all teachers including assistants should have an understanding of the developmental patterns of young children. Your child's teacher should have a sense of what expectations and behavior are appropriate at which ages, and when different types of materials should be introduced. Some of the larger early childhood schools have brochures or catalogs listing the teachers and their training. If a school does not have a catalog, be sure to ask the person who shows you the school about the teachers' backgrounds and training.

The National Daycare Study undertaken for the federal government in the 1970s found that one of the most important factors in the effectiveness of an early childhood school or day-care program was the training of the teachers. Ellen Galinsky reported on the study in her recent book: "In programs in which the teacher caregivers had early childhood training, the children behaved more positively and were more cooperative as well as more involved in the program. These children also made gains on standardized tests of learning."[2] It is of course important that a teacher's training is relevant to his or her work with young children and that the training was not just a few courses taken for credit and then forgotten, but rather part of a lifelong interest in new research and communication with fellow teachers.

Another important issue is the rate of teacher turnover. Some turnover is to be expected in early childhood schools since many teachers are young, the pay is low, and a number of teachers leave the profession after a few years. However, in schools that have been in existence for a number of years, there should be a sense of continuity. In the larger early childhood school serving a hundred or more students, there should be a core of teachers who have been at the school for five years or more. In a smaller school with fifty or fewer students, look for continuity in leadership of the school, and perhaps one or two teachers who have been there for three to five years.

•• Administrative Leadership

Administrative leadership was identified as the most important factor in a school by a large group of directors who responded to a survey done by Childcare Information Exchange, a magazine for directors of early childhood schools and day-care centers.

The head of the school, often known as the director, is a key element in the quality of an early childhood school. He or she sets the tone of the school by screening and hiring teachers and providing for their ongoing training. The head also communicates the goals and philosophy of the school to both teachers and prospective parents. The head should be someone whose opinions you respect and with whom you feel comfortable talking.

•• Class Size

A third important factor in the quality of a school is class size. The National Daycare Study also found that the number of children in a class was an important factor in the overall quality of their experience, as well as in the gains they made in standardized tests. The NAEYC recommends in its 1987 accreditation criteria and procedures that groups for two-year-olds contain between eight and ten children and no more than twelve. For three-year-olds, groups should be between fourteen and eighteen children, with twenty the largest acceptable size. For four- and five-year-olds, groups may have as many as sixteen to eighteen, but should not exceed twenty. The NAEYC believes that the optimal child/teacher ratio for two-year-olds is one to four or one to five; for three-year-olds, one to seven or one to eight; for four- or five-year-olds, one to eight or one to nine.[3]

•• Physical Layout

An early childhood school should be safe, clean, and cheerful. Studies have shown that increasing the number of children in a given space also increases the level of aggressiveness. The NAEYC recommends a minimum of 35 square feet of indoor usable playroom floor space per child, and a minimum of 75 square feet of outdoor space per child.[4] The space should be arranged so that it is easy for children to move around the room from one activity to another and to work either individually or in groups.

•• Health and Safety

The most basic and fundamental issue in any early childhood school is the health and safety of the children it serves. An early childhood school should be licensed or accredited by an appropriate local or state agency. Licensing standards vary from state to state, but most states have codes concerning fire protection, sanitation, water quality, and childhood immunizations. In some states, early childhood schools must be accredited as well as licensed. Since 1985 the National Academy of Early Childhood Programs, under the auspices of the NAEYC, has offered voluntary accreditation for schools that meet national standards in curriculum, staff-child and staff-parent interaction, staff qualifications and development, administration, staffing, physical environment, health and safety, nutrition and food service, and self-evaluation. The decision on accreditation is made by a commission of early childhood experts. A few early childhood schools have chosen instead to be accredited by the National Association of Independent Schools (NAIS). Both organizations have vigorous standards, and as long as one or the other does the accreditation, you can trust the conclusion.

Small schools with less than sixty students may decide not to bother going through the rather lengthy accreditation process. This does not necessarily mean the school is not one of quality, but it does mean that you should check the credentials of the teachers and administrators carefully and make sure all state and local licensing requirements have been met. Call your local health department for a list of requirements and ask if the schools you are considering meet these standards. When you visit a school, check to see that children arrive and leave in a safe and properly supervised manner, and ask if the school requires a parent's written authorization before releasing a child to anyone else. Look for teachers at the door. Look also for crossing guards. If there are driveways near either play areas or walkways, what precautions are taken to protect the children? All outside doors should be locked or supervised by a responsible person to ensure that strangers cannot wander in. Outdoor play areas should be well supervised and protected from the intrusion of unauthorized people. A school should also have a plan for dealing with medical emergencies; its policy should be to request written permission from parents for emergency treatment in the event that the parents cannot be reached.

It is also important that the school's policy on attendance in the case of minor illnesses be in line with your own feelings. Are you the kind of parent who believes all children get colds? Or do you get upset at the thought of your child being in a room with a bunch of other children with runny noses and coughs?

You might also want to think about how protective you are. How do you feel about your child falling on the stairs or on playground equipment? Do you feel the occasional fall, cut, or scrape is just part of growing up, or are you the kind of parent who says, as a number of parents have said to me, "I don't want my children going up and down stairs by themselves. The thought of having them fall scares me." There are no right and wrong feelings about this. What is important is that you, as the parent, feel comfortable with the balance of freedom and supervision a school gives your child.

•• Philosophy

For most parents it is important to have a sense of shared values with others connected with the school. Spend some time identifying your priorities, and compare them to those of other parents you may know with children in the school. Are the same things important to you that seem to be important to the other parents? Do you seem to share priorities and values? Values can be as basic as promptness and attendance during a minor illness or as philosophical as the role of competition or the importance of community service. For example, a parent who is also a teacher was brought up to believe that an 8:30 arrival really meant 8:30—not 8:35. "If school starts at 8:30, I'm trained to be there at 8:30. If I take my child to school I want to know the other parents share this idea of all starting the class at the same time so that the children who are there first thing aren't interrupted by the children who arrive late every single day."

In terms of social philosophy, many schools make a point of playing down competition—even in games—by emphasizing a cooperative team approach to problem solving rather than individual accomplishment. If your family is naturally very competitive and likes to play to win, your child may have difficulty reconciling two such different goals. Young children are generally happier when they see a general consistency between home and school. More than a few parents have said to me, "We have a very relaxed life at home without a lot of structure so I think my child should go to a school with plenty of structure to balance what they have at home." My experience argues that this is a mistake and only ends up confusing young children. Children are far more likely to thrive when the amount of order and structure at school is consistent with the amount of order and structure in their homes.

•• Financial Considerations

For many parents financial considerations play a role in the selection of an early childhood school. Costs vary depending both on where you live and on whether you want an extended-day, a full-day, or a half-day program. Some programs charge by the week, some by the month or by the term. Others ask parents to sign a contract for the year. In January 1990 the United States General Accounting Office estimated the yearly cost of a quality program accredited by NAEYC at $4,200.[5] Since then costs have risen and in some large cities—New York and Chicago, for example—parents tell me they expect to pay more than $7,000 a year for a full-time, quality early childhood school.

Early childhood schools run by religious groups sometimes have sliding fee scales depending on parental income. A few offer financial aid. Another option for some parents is a cooperative school. However, bear in mind that the reason cooperative schools are less expensive is that parents do a large percentage of the work themselves and all parents are expected to do their share. If you work full-time, a cooperative school may not be a realistic choice.

As a general rule it is not advisable to shop for bargains in early childhood schools. Quality education is expensive. While the most expensive school is not necessarily the best, schools with fees considerably below those of other schools in the same area may be cutting corners in ways that could be detrimental to your child's development and even safety.

•• Finding Early Childhood Schools

There are a variety of ways to find out about schools in your neighborhood. Since many early childhood schools are associated with churches, synagogues, YMCAs, or YMHAs, this is a good place to start your inquiries. Pediatricians are useful sources of information, and so are friends and colleagues with older children. To find out about public pre-K programs, call your local school district. Many communities have child-care resource and referral agencies (R&R) that provide information on early childhood schools. A number of large corporations also have R&R for employees. The National Association of Child Care Resource and Referral Agencies (see appendix) can give you information on referral services in your community. Finally, if you need more names, check the yellow pages of your phone book under "Schools—Nursery Schools and Kindergarten."

Remember, however, that no matter how reliable your source or how enthusiastically he or she praises a school, that school still may not be right for your child. Always check things out for yourself with a visit to the school.

••THE VISIT••

Most early childhood schools encourage parents to schedule a visit without their child to tour the school, visit classrooms, and see children working and playing. Watch carefully how the teachers interact with the children. Do they look at children when they are talking to them? Do they get down on the floor with the children so they are at eye level some of the time? Do the teachers seem warm and friendly? Do they seem to like the children and be genuinely interested in them? Do they really listen to the children, or do they seem to be only half-listening—perhaps because they are busy doing something else? Most teachers, like parents, occasionally find themselves trying to do half a dozen things all at the same time and you should not fault them for this. However, there should also be times when each child feels he or she has the teacher's undivided attention. Are the children encouraged to express their ideas and feelings? Do the teachers encourage language development by asking children open-ended questions that cannot be answered simply yes or no? Are the teachers reasonably articulate? Do they speak grammatically and use language well? Do they seem to be talking down to the children? How are the children disciplined? Do the teachers guide and redirect the children? Do they criticize? How do they deal with a child who refuses guidance and suggestions? Ask yourself whether you are comfortable with the way problems that arise in the classroom are handled. Are rules clear and consistently enforced? Do expectations for children's behavior seem appropriate for the children's age?

How do the children interact with each other? Are they learning to share and cooperate? Do they seem to like each other? Are they quarreling and fighting? How do the teachers handle aggression? And once again, are you comfortable with the way they handle it?

Do you get a sense of close communication and sharing between teachers and parents? Do the teachers seem happy to see parents at the beginning and end of the day and to share anecdotes and new accomplishments? Are there regularly scheduled conferences, as well as informal exchanges?

During your visit to each school the most important thing you can do is to keep your eyes and ears open. Ask yourself the following questions while you are there and able to observe the environment for yourself rather than later when you are at home and struggling to remember your impressions:

Physical Space

•• Are the rooms clean and bright and reasonably spacious?
•• Are the walls freshly painted?
•• Is the equipment clean and in good repair?

- • Is there an outdoor play area?
- • Is the space well set up for the children?

Educational Materials

- • Are there books and pictures and age-appropriate materials and toys around?
- • Are the materials well organized and readily available to the children?

One astute grandmother described a visit to her granddaughter's school, which, at first glance, seemed to be a well-equipped nursery school complete with a pet rabbit. But on closer observation things were not quite right. The books and materials were on high shelves out of reach of the children, and the rabbit was locked in a small, dirty cage that was shoved in a corner. The children had no opportunity to pet the rabbit and interact with it, or to learn anything about animal behavior.

Activities

- • Do the children seem busily involved and happy? Is there sparkle and enthusiasm? Are the children smiling?
- • Are the activities adult or child oriented? Is the emphasis on product or process?
- • Does the children's artwork appear to be individualized? Do all the art projects look the same—is everyone making an identical pumpkin for Halloween? Of course, it is important not to jump to conclusions here without first finding out the intentions of the teacher. Five similar-looking snowmen could be part of an exercise in following directions rather than artistic expression.

Staff

- • Do the children appear to like the teachers and treat them with respect?
- • Do the teachers seem genuinely interested in the children and do they treat them with respect? Do they try to facilitate interaction between the children?
- • Do the director and teachers seem to be the sort of people you would be comfortable working with?

Philosophy

•• Does the school seem to try to fit the needs of each individual child, or is it your sense that it attempts to fit each child into the school?

•• How diverse is the student body? Are you comfortable with the degree of diversity?

•• Does the school appear to do what it says it will do in the brochure or other written material? This can be a tough question and may require reflection after the visit.

•• Do you understand the admissions process? Are you comfortable with it? The way in which a school handles its admissions can give you a sense of its priorities and often reflects its character.

•• Do you have the sense that you are really seeing the school as it is, or are you seeing just what the admissions office wants you to see?

•• Is the school open about its shortcomings as well as its virtues?

•• And, finally, does it feel right to you? Is this the kind of place to which you would be happy bringing your child every morning?

After you have asked yourself these questions, you may want to ask the school some of the following questions:

•• What is the background and level of experience of the faculty?

•• What is the rate of faculty turnover?

•• How diverse is the student body? The faculty?

•• When does the school year begin and end?

•• How long are vacations? Which religious holidays are observed?

•• Is the program full-day or half-day? What are the hours? Do they offer an extended-day option?

•• Describe a typical day.

•• How much time do children spend in group activities versus independent activities?

•• Are children grouped developmentally or chronologically?

•• How many openings are anticipated for your child's age group?

•• Are children accepted on a first-come, first-served basis, or is there a screening process?

•• Is there financial aid? On what basis is it awarded?

•• Are there age cutoffs for entrance? If so, what are they?

•• Will your child be one of the younger or one of the older children in the class?

•• To what extent does the school welcome children with learning problems? What kind of resources does it have to deal with them?

•• How is a child disciplined when he or she disobeys or acts out in the classroom?

•• How does the school handle separation? Is a parent permitted to stay in the classroom? For how long? (See chapter 4 for a discussion of separation issues.)

•• What are the opportunities and expectations for parent involvement? Are there any requirements? Does the school expect a greater time commitment than you can reasonably make? This can be a problem for working parents, particularly in schools run on a cooperative basis. Some schools have more appreciation than others of the needs of working parents, and acknowledge that they are not always available to come to the school during working hours.

•• What kinds of parent-teacher contacts are encouraged?

•• Is the school affiliated with any religious organization? What does this affiliation mean? Is there any required participation in religious services or instruction?

•• What are the expectations for students as they get older?

•• What schools do children go on to for kindergarten and first grade?

•• Is there bus service?

•• Does the school offer after-school or summer programs? If both parents are working, it may be important to find a school with interesting activities after school hours.

After your visit, sit down and quietly go over all your impressions. If you know other parents with children in the school, talk to them about their experience. Ask them what they feel the school's strengths and weaknesses are, and whether or not they would pick the same school for a second child. But remember that their children may be very different from yours and their experience may not necessarily be yours. Trust your own initial feelings and impressions. If you feel uncomfortable with a school, don't choose it for your child no matter how enthusiastic your friends may be about it. Also remember that in many communities there are a number of good early childhood schools, any one of which could give your child an excellent start. And there is never one school that is the only right one for your child.

•• Children with Special Needs

Many early childhood schools save a few places for children with special needs. If your child has special needs, it is important that you discuss them openly with the school you are interested in to make sure the school has the training and staff to give your child the help he or she needs. Public Law 94-142, the Education for All Handicapped Children Act, gives each state the responsibility for identifying, screening, evaluating, and providing appropriate educational services for all children with learning problems from kindergarten on up. Some school districts offer preschool programs under the federally funded Chapter I Program for low-income families. Your child could be eligible for a Chapter I preschool program even if you do not qualify as low-income if your local public school participates in the program. Parents should call either the board of education or the special education department in your school district for information about local programs and eligibility requirements.

•• Alternatives to Early Childhood School

••PARENT-CHILD ACTIVITIES••

You may decide not to send your children to early childhood school because you cannot find a quality school near you or simply because you want to have your children at home with you. If you want to keep your two- or three-year-old at home, by all means do so. Your children are only going to be this age once, and you will never be able to change your mind and turn the clock back. If your children have space to play and explore, opportunities to be with other children, and caring adults to help them discover and define their world; if your children seem happy and fulfilled at home, and full of zest and joy of life; and if you yourself are content to have them at home, then relax and enjoy this time together. Your children will not grow up less intelligent or knowledgeable. They will learn from the conversations and experiences you have together, and they will grow up with the memories of the special time you have shared. Your children may initially have less experience in taking turns, following directions, relating to different adults, and getting along with children in a group, but there are alternative ways for you to introduce your children to group activities and help them learn social skills.

Alternatives to early childhood school include parent-run play groups, parent-child classes at the local Y or community center, and parent-child classes at gymnasiums and museums. Many of these classes are excellent and, provided you don't over-schedule your child, they can be a fine way for your child to get used to being with other children and doing things together in a group. Your child can gain experience in relating to other adults and begin to see adults as important sources of information and assistance. Perhaps most importantly, the classes give you and your child the chance to get out of the house and do something enjoyable together. Some classes run either on weekends or in the early evening to accommodate the needs of working parents. It doesn't really matter a great deal whether you and your child pick an art class, a music class, or a gym class. The important thing is that you both enjoy what you are doing and that your child has the opportunity to interact with other children and adults.

••PLAY GROUPS••

Another good alternative to early childhood school is a parent-run play group. Four or five neighborhood parents with children of roughly the same age get together once or twice a week for an hour or so. In some groups, the parents take turns having all the children play together in their house; in other groups the parents prefer to use a neutral space in a neighborhood house, church, or synagogue. If a neutral space is available, I recommend taking advantage of it. Two- and three-year-olds usually feel very possessive about their rooms and their toys and may see other children as unwelcome intruders. If you have to use one of your homes, pick a neutral space such as a dining room rather than your child's room, and keep a special set of toys that are brought out only for the play group. Most successful play groups have some well-planned short periods of structured activities that bring the children together in a group. Typically one parent takes responsibility for each session and plans group games, songs, or simple art projects for part of the play group. Such group activities are important because preschool-age children are just beginning to be able to play together. Much of their play is still what is known as *parallel play*, with two or more children playing by themselves without interacting with the children next to them. (For a more thorough discussion of the developmental abilities of children at different ages, see chapter 4.)

Parents often benefit from being a part of a play group as much as their children do. One mother who lives in a rural area said to me, "We started out with a few moms saying, 'Let's get together so the children can play and we can talk.' It was important for us to get together so we could talk to other mothers about our children and share ideas on how to cope with problems. It seemed to make us feel less isolated somehow." When parents move to a new community, becoming part of a play group is one of the best ways of making contact with other parents with young children.

•• Conclusion

The decision to send your children to early childhood school is a very personal one. There are no universal right or wrong answers. However, if you do decide you want to send your child to early childhood school, it is important that your needs and desires coincide with the school's. You will need to be familiar with the school's admissions procedures and understand how its decisions are made. In chapter 3, we will look at some of the factors schools consider in making admissions decisions, and we will explore your own role in getting your child into the early childhood school of your choice.

•• •• •• ••
THREE
•• •• •• •• •• •• •• •• •• •• •• ••

Getting In: A Parent's Guide to Admissions

The September before my own son James turned two, I started thinking about sending him to early childhood school. All James's friends from our mother-child play group were going. I thought it would be good for James to have a place to go that was all his own where he could play and explore and make friends with children his own age. As an educator, I was familiar with most of the early childhood schools in the area. I chose three schools that I felt had provided a particularly fine early childhood experience for my former students and that were also reasonably near our home. I called a few friends who were teaching kindergarten and first grade in ongoing schools to confirm that my perceptions were still correct. Then I called the schools and made appointments to visit. My husband and I applied to all three, toured the schools, met the directors, and took our son for interviews. In each school the process differed slightly, but at all the schools we were impressed with the warm, friendly atmosphere and with the genuine interest expressed in us and in our son.

We visited the first school just before Halloween. My son became frightened by some life-size masks hanging on the wall and screamed for the first five minutes of the interview. At the next school, he insisted that I sit on the floor beside him while he drew pictures and built towers out of blocks. At the third school, he was asked what noise a duck makes and what happens to leaves in the fall. He refused to answer. Despite all my years of teaching, I knew—like all mothers—that my son was the cleverest and most precocious toddler to walk across the threshold of any early childhood school and, despite all my

•• •• •• ••

training in child development, I desperately wanted him to demonstrate his talents. Somehow I managed to keep silent and not suggest that he recite the nursery rhymes he said to himself before going to sleep at night, or count to ten as his grandfather had taught him to do, or even share the Spanish he had picked up from the baby-sitter. Despite his refusal to volunteer any of these unique talents and his insistence on behaving instead like an ordinary almost two-year-old, my son, like his friends from the play group, was admitted to all three schools.

Less than two years later the baby boom hit. The schools were overrun with two-year-olds, and there were not enough places in toddler programs for all of them. At a time when many secondary schools were having trouble filling their classrooms because of declining enrollment, neither the early childhood schools nor their admissions directors were prepared for the sudden onslaught of applicants. My son's school was forced to stop accepting applications for the next year on the first of October because it didn't have the staff to interview any more applicants. This situation continues today in certain areas. In some larger cities, the tight admissions situation has been accentuated by parents' applying to as many as ten early childhood schools out of fear that there will be no room for their child in any school. This has made things more difficult both for parents and for the schools, which often have little idea how many of their applications are serious. One admissions director at an early childhood school notes, "It isn't so much the number of applicants as the number of applications that has increased so dramatically."

The admissions picture for early childhood school can vary widely from year to year, and from school to school, even in the same general geographical area. Some schools may be actively seeking to fill empty spots, while others are bombarded with more applications than they can even begin to process. A school may have space for three-year-olds but not for toddlers, or vice versa. But unlike the lines outside a popular restaurant, the number of applicants does not necessarily equate with the quality of a school or its appropriateness for you and your child.

•• Publicly Financed Programs

Some public school districts have experimental pre-K programs, and as we discussed earlier, there are a number of publicly financed early childhood intervention programs. However, because most publicly funded programs try to determine physical, social, economic, and educational needs as criteria for selection, these programs are often limited to low-income families or children with special needs.[1]

Head Start, one of the best-known intervention programs for children between the ages of three and five, was established specifically for the benefit of low-income families. Space in Head Start is so limited, however, that educators estimate that it is currently available to less than 20 percent of the children eligible for it. Individual Head Start programs develop plans for recruiting and selecting children under HEW guidelines. Enrollment must reflect the racial and ethnic balance of disadvantaged families in the area. Children are assigned to programs based on an assessment of family situation, age, handicaps, developmental level, health, or learning problems. Ninety percent of the children in a Head Start program must come from families with incomes below the federal poverty guidelines. Ten percent of the children must be handicapped. Low-income handicapped children are given priority.

Preschool programs in public schools usually exist only as a result of initiatives by the local community school district. In some states funds are available on a competitive basis for experimental pre-K programs designed for three- and four-year-olds from low-income families. There are also grants for so-called umbrella programs—innovative pilot projects to meet special local needs. These needs might include a preschool program for gifted children, an after-school program, or a parents co-op. Pre-K programs may also be funded by an individual state legislator's discretionary funds. Other programs are funded through Chapter I, according to federal guidelines, for "low achieving children in low-income areas."

Two of the more successful publicly funded preschool programs have been Project Giant Step in New York City and Smart Start in Massachusetts. Eligibility for Project Giant Step is based on a combination of social and financial considerations, and approximately one out of five disadvantaged four-year-olds in the city participates in the program. Senator Edward Kennedy has called Smart Start his "top educational priority," and proponents of Smart Start hope to make preschool education available to every child whose family wants it, regardless of economic resources. According to Senator Kennedy, this is an "education program, a day-care program, a job program, a literacy program, a health-care program, a dropout program, and an anti-crime and drug abuse program."[2] Elsewhere in Massachusetts, local school committees have authorized transition-to-kindergarten programs, which are partially funded by fees from parents. Scholarship assistance for families with financial need is available through the public schools of these communities. Before being admitted to transition programs, children are interviewed by the early childhood education coordinator to evaluate their readiness for the program. If children are deemed ready, admission is on a first-come, first-served basis. School districts in a number of states run summer programs to get children used to being in school and to introduce them to age-appropriate activities and skills. All children who will attend kindergarten in the district in September are usually eligible for the summer sessions. There are also a variety of special preschool programs for three- and four-year-olds who suffer severe developmental delays and for handicapped children referred by pediatricians. A number of states are experimenting with arrangements with private nursery schools and developmentally oriented day-care centers to allow more low-income children the benefit of early childhood school experiences. And one school district in Milwaukee has entered into contracts with private day-care centers to provide both child care and kindergarten to disadvantaged four- and five-year-olds.

Despite the recent increase in publicly financed preschool programs, there is still a lack of widely available public programs for children before kindergarten. However, if you think your child might be eligible for one of the publicly financed programs, contact your local board of education for information on programs in your district.

•• Private Early Childhood Schools

Because most publicly funded programs are limited to low-income families, many families must seek alternatives in private schools. Private early childhood schools are often located in churches or synagogues. Some schools are part of national chains such as Kindercare or Children's World. Businesses sometimes run schools that combine early childhood school and daycare for their employees. These schools may accept neighborhood children on a space-available basis, and places are often eagerly sought. Several months before it opened there were already more than a hundred names on a waiting list for places in a school run by the developer of Heller Industrial Park in New Jersey. A few schools are affiliated with universities and are run as lab schools to test new educational theories and to train student teachers. Places here, again, are few and usually in great demand. Other early childhood schools are not separate schools at all, as we saw earlier, but divisions of ongoing schools. It is always a good idea to apply to more than one school. If the admissions situation seems to be particularly tight and you live in a large city, you might want to apply to as many as six.

If you are interested in a particular school, I recommend you call the admissions office and try to get a realistic idea of how many available spots the school actually has. Schools do not volunteer or publicly announce that information. One parent described this situation to me: "They were marching all these parents through the school and, if you were going on the basis of the tour, you would assume they were going to double the class of three-year-olds. It turned out that because they already had two sections of toddlers who would be going on to the three-year-old program, they had only eight openings: four for boys, and four for girls. They already knew they had some sibling applicants that they were going to have to take, and I remember sitting there thinking, 'This is pretty misleading for parents.' " Some programs that begin with infants and combine early childhood school and daycare as the children get older may be so small that they only take four infants a year. One teacher told me, "As soon as a mom gets pregnant she puts herself on a waiting list."

•• First Come, First Served

Many early childhood schools admit children on the basis of chronological age or date of application—a first-come, first-served approach. Dates for application vary greatly from one part of the country to another. In some towns you may be able to sign up during the September your child begins. A few schools are very flexible and accept applications throughout the year. Other popular schools stop accepting applications almost a year before a child would expect to begin. These schools are not trying to make things difficult for parents. They realize that they can give only a certain number of applications the kind of time and individual attention they deserve. The mother of a four-year-old recalls that when she began looking at programs in July, she was horrified to find that everything was full and her daughter had to be put on a waiting list. The next year she moved to another town only to discover that the available slots filled up by May. Another mother recounted her reaction to admissions deadlines: "This was my first child and I didn't know that you had to apply so far ahead of time. I called in February and found it was already too late. But we were lucky because the school called back three days later and said that they had a place for Nicholas." There are usually a few last-minute vacancies, but it is a good idea to plan ahead and apply ten to twelve months before your child is due to start.

••Age Cutoffs••

When you apply to a school, be sure to ask about age cutoffs. Some early childhood schools require that a child be three by June 1; others may accept children with September birthdays. Some schools insist that a child be toilet trained, others do not. In certain classes you will find that all the children have birthdays within a few months of each other, while other schools accommodate a wider age range within their groups. One mother expected that her third child would automatically follow her two older daughters to early childhood school, only to discover to her dismay that her last daughter missed the age cutoff by a month.

••Screening Applicants

Some schools, usually in large cities, do not accept children on a first-come, first-served basis. Instead, they try to make an assessment of both a child's readiness and the parents' compatibility with the school's particular program. These schools may use a variety of screening methods to make this assessment. The screening process usually includes an interview with both parents after they have had a tour of the school, and a subsequent meeting with the child. Schools interview parents because they are looking for a good match for their school. They are looking for parents who understand the school and will feel comfortable there. With very young children, unless the child has an obvious behavior problem or severe developmental deficit, the parent interview and questionnaire are often more important than the observation of the child. Some schools admit children solely on the basis of parent interviews and questionnaires without actually meeting the child. In general, in the admissions process for older children, more emphasis is placed on the child's own demonstrated abilities and talents, but at the early childhood level schools are every bit as interested in you as in your child.

••THE APPLICATION••

Schools usually ask parents to complete an application that contains questions about them and their child. The questions range from simple queries about allergies and medications to those that require more in-depth descriptions of your child's likes and dislikes, fears or anxieties, bedtime rituals, relationships with siblings, and responses to separation. It is often a good idea to look over your child's baby book before filling out an application or going to a parent interview. Many schools will want to know about the course of your pregnancy and whether your child was premature. They may ask questions about your child's developmental history: When did your daughter first crawl? Did she crawl forward or backward first? When did your son start to talk? What was his first word? His first phrase? Most schools will ask who cares for the child during the day and whether there are other adults such as grandparents, a housekeeper, or a nanny living in the household. Schools usually want to know whether a child has experienced any significant illnesses, traumatic experiences, or health problems. Some schools inquire whether there is any family history of learning problems. A school may also ask you to describe your child's personality, give examples of the ways he or she likes to spend time, and explain how anger or frustration is usually expressed at home and what kind of discipline you find most effective. Schools that don't ask these questions on the application may well ask them later during the parent interview. It is best to answer all questions simply and honestly without either putting your child down or trying to prove that he or she is a prodigy.

••LETTERS OF RECOMMENDATION••

Some schools may ask for the names of several people who know your family well. A few schools ask you to have one or two of these people write a letter. When a school asks for recommendations, it is important to remember that they want to find out as much as they can about you and your child, about your values and goals, and about how you function as a family. They are not interested in how many famous people you know.

••THE PARENT INTERVIEW••

Parents are usually asked to meet either alone or in small groups with the head of the school or with the admissions director. The meeting may last anywhere from twenty minutes to an hour. Sometimes the child may be in the room playing while the parents talk. The head or the admissions director describes the school and explains its philosophy and goals. He or she may ask the parents specific questions about their child's interests, habits, likes, and dislikes. The parents, in turn, have an opportunity to ask questions about the school.

During the parent interview, schools are interested in:

1. Family dynamics. Do parents interact in a positive way with each other and with their child?
2. Whether the parents really seem to know their child. Are their expectations realistic?
3. How parents deal with separation issues. (See chapter 4 for a discussion of separation.)
4. How the parents react if their child misbehaves. Do they set limits? Are they firm as well as sympathetic, or do they throw up their hands and try to pretend it isn't happening?
5. The level of love and trust between parent and child. Does the child look to the parents for encouragement and guidance?
6. Whether the goals of parents and school are compatible. If there is a discrepancy in values, will the child be confused?
7. Whether the parents will trust and support the school.
8. Whether the parents and school will be able to pull together for the benefit of the child.

The interview process can be a shock to a parent. One mother remarked to me after an interview, "They ended up interviewing me most of the time. I felt like I was the candidate. They didn't spend much time observing my son; they didn't even seem to be trying to get a sense of him. The whole emphasis was on whether there was a good fit between the school and the kind of education we wanted for our son."

Try not to let yourself be intimidated by the process. Remember that most admissions directors are parents or grandparents. They have been in your shoes themselves. As one admissions director, whose own son was turned down for admission to six nursery schools and is now an honor student at an Ivy League college, said, "We have all been through this ourselves—we've seen it from the other side. We understand your apprehension and we realize how much you want the best for your child."

••THE CHILD'S INTERVIEW••

Many early childhood schools will also want to see your child either with or without you. This interview is not nearly as bad as it sounds. Schools are not looking for "the perfect child," nor have they been secretly commissioned to search out future Nobel Prize winners. The child's interview is a way for the school to get to know your child, to get a sense of your child's learning style and readiness for a particular program. A recent panel of admissions directors reassured its audience of anxious parents that they fully expected each child to act like a typical two-, three-, or four-year-old. A father reported to me, "The whole idea of going through an interview at that age [two] was appalling, but the fact is it was fun while Andrew was there and not at all anxiety producing."

Mitten Wainwright, the director of Park Avenue Christian Church Day School in New York and an early childhood educator for more than twenty years, says, "We don't worry about natural disasters like a young child throwing up, or wetting his pants, or refusing to come in the room because he thinks it's a doctor's office. What we're really interested in is not what happens but how the parent handles it. Do they get all upset at the child or do they take it in stride."

••WHAT TO TELL YOUR CHILD BEFORE
THE INTERVIEW••

Parents often ask me what they should say to their child before the interview. Several longtime admissions directors have suggested that parents might tell their toddler, "You are going to meet a lady. She is called a teacher and she likes to play with children. I've met her and I think she's a very nice person. I want you to come and meet her too. She will share some toys with you and you'll have a chance to play with her, and she will show you some new ways to play with her toys. Mommy and Daddy will be there with you."

But before you say anything to your child, find out from each school exactly how your child's interview will be handled. Then tell your child in advance whether you will be in the room or not; whether there will be a tour of the school; and, perhaps most important from the child's point of view, whether there will be toys and a chance to play with other children. Again it is probably a good idea to take notes during your conversation with the school about these details since, as I mentioned earlier, the process is slightly different in each school. If you tell your daughter she will play in a classroom with other children and in that particular school the child goes off to another room alone with a teacher, with not a child or toy in sight; or if you tell your son not to worry, Mommy will be right there, and then he is whisked away at the door, you are setting the stage for problems. Misinformation can be very upsetting for a child.

••WHAT WILL HAPPEN AT THE INTERVIEW?••

One mother gave this description of her daughter's interview: "My daughter was invited to join a group of children in the class. There were a variety of play materials around the room. She moved among the group of children freely and played with the materials. The director talked to us and to her at the same time, but I had a very distinct feeling that she was assessing Sarah's readiness."

Another mother remembers that while she was talking to the admissions director, her son walked around the room. "Various materials had been set out and Charles was free to participate in whatever activity interested him: petting the rabbit, working on a puzzle, building with blocks. No one asked him to do anything, they just let him do what he pleased, but it was clear to me that they were watching what he was doing. As we were getting ready to leave, the teacher remarked, 'Oh isn't that wonderful how well he holds onto things.' So she was indeed looking at Charles's readiness."

At another school, a parent recalls that the interview was conducted during the tour of the school and the admissions director seemed "to be more interested in Elizabeth's relationship with my husband and me than she was in her reactions to the things going on in the school. At the next school we visited, the interview was very structured. Elizabeth was one-on-one with a teacher doing a series of directed activities while we watched from another part of the room."

During most interviews for early childhood school, children are observed in small groups of five or six for thirty to forty minutes. They are given the opportunity to interact with each other and with two or three early childhood teachers, as well as with a variety of materials designed for young children. These materials may include simple puzzles, Play-Doh, Legos, blocks, paper and crayons, cars and trucks, dolls, cups and plates, and other play equipment from the housekeeping corner. At some point children are usually given a simple snack consisting of either fruit or cheese and crackers and juice. Teachers often use this time to get a sense of children's socialization skills as well as how adept they are at drinking from a cup and feeding themselves.

Teachers usually spend a few minutes talking to each child individually to get a sense of language development and how well the child expresses his or her ideas. Some schools structure interviews so that children are doing a series of directed activities alone with a teacher. These activities are often loosely based on Gesell's developmental schedules and may include such activities as building towers out of blocks, matching shapes, and naming objects. It is important for parents to remember that these activities are being used to help the school assess a child's developmental readiness and learning style, not the child's IQ (intelligence quotient). A child's developmental age (DA) is the age at which the child is functioning socially, emotionally, intellectually, and physically. Developmental age is a qualitative rather than a quantitative concept. It is not a numerical score but rather a series of observations on the way a child functions. Psychologists at the Gesell Institute stress that there are no right or wrong answers on a developmental assessment. Instead, a child's responses are that child's way of exploring, ordering, solving, creating, and predicting his or her world. Responses not only show something of what a child knows and understands but also reflect that child's self-concept and learning style. How accurate the assessment is depends on the experience and skill of the evaluator. You should never consider one developmental assessment a definitive statement on your child.

What Is Being Evaluated at the Early Childhood Level?

As the teachers watch the children interacting with each other and with the materials, they notice:

1. The children's response to each other.
2. Their response to the materials.
3. Their physical behavior and expressions.
4. Their language use, and whether their language is sufficient to communicate their needs.
5. Their approaches to problem solving.
6. Their motor control, both large and small.
7. Their tolerance for frustration.
8. Their ability both to focus on a task and to handle transitions between activities.
9. Their sense of confidence and security.
10. Their interest in exploring and interacting with the environment.

··TESTS··

Formal tests are seldom used to assess the readiness of normal children with no suspected deficits for early childhood programs prior to kindergarten. Many educators agree with Dr. Margaret M. Devine, former president of the World Organization for Early Childhood Education: "Children this age are essentially not testable" because they have difficulty understanding directions and do not take tests seriously. Tests are generally used only when problems or developmental gaps are suspected and to identify children who may need further evaluation and perhaps special help.

Tests are also occasionally used for admission to certain gifted and talented programs that begin before kindergarten. The most commonly used test for these programs is the Stanford-Binet, Fourth Edition, an IQ test which, unlike a readiness assessment, gives numerical scores and seeks to predict how well a child will actually perform in school. If IQ tests are used, they are generally used in conjunction with parent interviews and informal assessments of the child.

•• How Early Childhood Schools Decide

When schools make admissions decisions on other than a first-come, first-served basis, they usually give preference to the siblings of children already in the school and to the children of alumni/alumnae. If a school is affiliated with a church or synagogue, it will generally give preference to members of the congregation. Some ongoing schools give preference in their early childhood divisions to children they believe will remain through the elementary years.

It is important for parents to realize that early childhood schools are not looking for a class made up of child prodigies or academic superstars. Mary Solow, who has been involved in education for twenty-five years and is currently the director of Central Synagogue Nursery School, said to me, "We're not looking for the brightest and most beautiful. We are hoping that children will be relatively emotionally healthy and normal, and that their parents will be cooperative and supportive of our school. We care a lot about social kindness and decency and sharing. We know that not every child is going to be an A in physical and verbal development at age two or three. We're not looking for a class of geniuses. We make it clear from the beginning that we don't expect children to be able to say their ABCs or count to ten."

When they put together classes, early childhood schools first need to balance the ratio of girls and boys. Some like to have a mix of first, second, and third children as well as only children. Some look for a diversity of personality types and learning styles. Some look for children they feel will fit in comfortably both with the program and with other children in the class. Some try in a variety of ways, as we have seen, to assess children's developmental level and readiness for their program. Schools also look for the children they believe will benefit most from their program and who, by being part of a class, will in turn benefit the other children.

Most schools also look for parents they feel will be supportive of the school and be comfortable there, parents who seem to understand what the school stands for and who share its goals. They want parents who will be involved in school activities, will come to chapel in the morning if it is a church school, will help in the library and on trips, and will work with the teachers. Schools usually look for a certain amount of ethnic and economic diversity in the parent body, though this is generally not as great a factor at the early childhood level as later on.

••Who Makes the Decision?••

At the early childhood level, admissions decisions are usually made by the head of the school and, if the school is large enough to have one, the director of admissions.

••Waiting to Hear••

Several months or more may go by after you complete the application process before the school indicates whether or not your child has been accepted. One realistic father said to me, "I remember kind of sadly the anxiety a lot of people had when we were waiting to hear from schools. It reminded me too much of being a senior in high school waiting to hear from the colleges. Given the choices, at age two or three I don't think the stakes are that high—it's not like finding out if you're about to be drafted or something. Try to relax a little and have faith in your kids. They'll make out okay."

On the day my own daughter heard from her early childhood school, she and I were at a class at the Y. The two-year-olds were making tea and building castles. Their mothers were clustered by the puzzles. "I hate siblings," said one. "It's just not fair to the only child," said another. "I've been watching the mail every day, but nothing's come. And I don't even know whether that's good or bad," said a third. "You'll know by the envelope if she's been accepted," interjected the first mother. "Acceptances are always thick and businesslike. Rejections are thin and polite." The third mother sighed: "There's nothing to do but wait. It's like that stock market theory, the random walk selection; they put all the names up on the wall, close their eyes and throw darts. If they hit you, you're in, if not you're out."

On the way home that day, I reflected that not long before I had been on the other side of the admissions folder. As head of a junior school and a member of the admissions committee at a boys' school in New York, I had studied IQ scores and the results of screening tests that purportedly predicted future academic success as well as readiness for first grade. I had visited many different early childhood schools. I had watched children draw pictures and name objects and hop on one foot. I had listened to them tell their favorite stories. I had watched them at work and play in their classrooms, and I had read their early childhood school reports. I had met their parents and talked to their teachers. My colleagues and I had made our decisions and waited to see if they were right. The classes I helped put together were much like early childhood school classes. The children certainly weren't all geniuses, child prodigies, developmentally advanced, or always well behaved. The parents weren't all rich, or poor, or smart, or social, or talented; nor did they fit into any other simple category. The only common denominator I could find was that they all cared about their children's education enough to invest a considerable amount of time and money in it. They cared enough to get their children to school at eight-thirty every morning, to come to parents' nights and conferences, and to sit at miniature desks helping teachers make supplementary materials to use in the classroom. They were willing to work harder than average at being parents.

And what of the children themselves, the ones who were accepted—what would happen to them? According to the reports on their predecessors in the alumni notes, some would make it to the secondary school and college of their choice and others would not. Some would succeed in the eyes of the world or in their own secret dreams, and others would wish at fifty that they could start over again. All in all, they were probably very much like the children who ended up on the waiting list or the children who got the thin envelopes. Whether or not they ever got into the early childhood school of their choice, they would grow up and find jobs, get married, have children, and worry about where their own children were going to go to school.

When we got home, as I lifted my daughter out of her stroller

49

I noticed a thick envelope outside the front door. I breathed a sigh of relief.

••THE WAIT LIST••

The meaning of a wait list varies greatly from school to school. One school director told me, "I can't bear to send a rejection letter to the parents of a two-year-old, so we just put them all on the wait list even though we know we're never going to take them." Other schools feel it is fairer to put only those children on the wait list whom they plan to accept if there is an opening. If your child is put on a wait list and you are interested in the school, call the school, tell them how much you like the school, and try to get a realistic sense of what the chances are that a place might open up.

••If Your Child Does Not Get into the School You Want

No matter how smart and attractive your child is or what great parents you are, your child may well be turned down at several schools if you live in a large urban area with a fast-growing population of two- or three-year-olds. As Reveta Bowers, director of children's programs at the Center for Early Education in Los Angeles, said recently, "I tell parents that if your child doesn't get into this school, it does not necessarily reflect on your child. It does not mean that we found something lacking in your child. It does not mean that your child isn't smart and accomplished and well-rounded. It just means there are lots of smart and accomplished and well-rounded children and unfortunately we don't have the room to accommodate the large numbers that are seeking admission to our programs." Do not take a rejection letter from an early childhood school personally, and above all don't let it influence your feelings toward your child. Remember, your child is still his or her own wonderful, adorable, funny, and sometimes exasperating self, and your life together goes on with all its marvelous and awful moments still intact. Try to put the experience with the school behind you with the realization that no matter how much you thought you liked that school, it probably wasn't right for you and your child after all. Turn your attention to the schools where your child has been accepted. If you are still not sure which one would be the best choice, ask to visit again before making a decision. You may also want to spend some time reflecting on whether your child is ready for early childhood school or would benefit from waiting a year. In the next chapter we will look at the meaning of readiness and explore some of the ways readiness is assessed in young children.

·· ·· ·· ··
F O U R
·· ·· ·· ·· ·· ·· ·· ·· ·· ·· ·· ··

Parents and Children:
Ready or Not

Children are ready for school when they have a basic sense of trust, a sense that no matter what happens they will be taken care of—they will be safe. Then they are able to separate from their parents and enter a relationship with other people in a new environment with new materials. If a child has trust, anything else can be taught.

ALEXANDRA ZIMMER,
FORMER DIRECTOR, THE MADISON
AVENUE PRESBYTERIAN DAY
SCHOOL, NEW YORK CITY

The idea that children should be "ready" for early childhood school is relatively new. The word *ready* comes from the Anglo-Saxon and originally pertained to riding, not school. Educators first began to apply the term readiness to children in the late 1920s and early 1930s as a result of studies by Dr. Arnold Gesell, founder of the Guidance Nursery at Yale. Gesell believed that each child passes through fixed developmental stages that are not necessarily related to the child's chronological age. Rather, each child progresses through each stage at his or her own rate. Any attempt to train a child to sit, talk, or read before that child was developmentally ready was useless, and perhaps even harmful.

For many years the consensus among educators was that intelligence was based almost solely on a child's genetic inheritance, and hence was not greatly influenced by either environment or early childhood education. In the late 1930s, at the Iowa Child Welfare Research Station, Harold Skeels and other researchers challenged these assumptions on the fixed nature of

·· ·· ·· ··

intelligence in their work with mentally handicapped children. In the 1960s Benjamin Bloom at the University of Chicago found that intelligence could be significantly influenced by a child's environment and early education. The debate on the relative importance of genetics versus environment goes on, as yet unresolved. However, educators now consider that opportunities to explore, to learn new skills, to solve problems, to express oneself verbally, and to make one's likes and dislikes known with words are vitally important for all young children. Educators such as Jean Piaget and Jerome Bruner have described a child's development as a careful balance between genetic inheritance and environment—a balance that can ultimately be controlled by a child's own actions. Just as a child's biological time clock cannot and should not be rushed, we cannot alter the rate at which that child passes through the progressive developmental stages. However, most of us, parents and educators alike, now believe that a child's overall development can be enhanced by providing appropriate challenges when he or she is ready to respond to them. But which challenges are appropriate at which ages? And how do we know when an individual child is ready to respond to them?

In attempting to answer these questions, many educators maintain that there is no such thing as general readiness, only the readiness of a particular child for a particular early childhood school. Some argue that it is even a contradiction to speak of a child's readiness for a particular school since a good early childhood school should be flexible enough to meet the needs of each individual child. They stress that it is important to fit the school to the child rather than the child to the school. Other educators believe that, despite the flexibility of teachers and the child-centered nature of a school, there are nevertheless certain minimal social and verbal skills a child needs to be comfortable in an early childhood school and to benefit from all the social, emotional, and cognitive challenges.

As we look at the developmental factors that seem to indicate readiness for early childhood school, it is important to remember that no two children are alike and that each child will have his or her own timetable for reaching each developmental milestone. Birth order and family size can also influence a child's readiness for early childhood school. Some early childhood teachers find that the only child and the firstborn child may initially have a slightly harder time adjusting to school than other children. And Dr. Nina Lief, director of the Early Childhood Development Center of the Center for Comprehensive Health Practice, an affiliate of New York Medical College, observes that at school children from very large families often choose to play alone rather than interacting with the other children in a group, if older brothers and sisters tend to intrude on their play space at home. If your child does not seem to be ready according to the criteria I discuss, this does not necessarily mean that you should not send your child to early childhood school, but rather that you will want to choose the school very carefully. You will want to look for a particularly flexible school that is sensitive to the individual needs of each child. You may also want to look for one that mixes children of different ages together rather than one that groups children by chronological age.

As we think about our children's readiness for school, it is important to remember that research has shown that a child's developmental level bears no direct relation to that child's intelligence. A child can be of average intelligence and developmentally quite advanced. Conversely, a child can be highly intelligent and still lag behind peers in some areas of development. Researchers at the Gesell Institute have found, however, that most children do better in school if they are grouped by developmental age rather than by either chronological or intellectual age.

·· Sending Your Child to School at Two

A two-year-old is an explorer who loves to touch, taste, smell, and feel everything in sight. Many two-year-olds like water- and sand-play. They delight in filling pails with water or small stones. Both boys and girls like to play with dolls and stuffed animals and imitate daily activities such as taking a bath or going to bed. Many children this age are fascinated by books and enjoy carrying them around. They often want adults to read favorite stories over and over again. Most two-year-olds can walk and run easily. Some can also walk up and down stairs and kick a ball. Two-year-olds love naming things and can use simple three-word sentences. They are usually able to ask for the things they

55

need, and some have a vocabulary of several hundred words. They can build a tower of six or seven blocks, string large beads, unscrew lids, manipulate Play-Doh, and paint and crayon. Many enjoy playing alongside other children in a style of play known as parallel play. Louise Bates Ames and her colleagues at the Gesell Institute say that the expression "terrible twos" is a misnomer since the average two-year-old is "a creature of considerable good will, quite willing and able to conform to the demands of those around him [her]."[1]

It is, rather, the two-and-a-half-year-old who is in a stage of disequilibrium. Ames finds that many two-and-a-half-year-olds are for a brief time "terrible and life is full of opposite extremes." Children this age can seem bossy and demanding. They often resent change and like to have familiar routines rigidly adhered to. While many begin to talk to other children, as well as to adults, most of their interactions with other children are negative. They aren't ready to share their possessions. There is usually a good deal of pushing and hitting when two-and-a-half-year-olds get together, and a lot of adult supervision is needed.[2]

Child-care experts agree that two-year-olds who are developing normally and have loving, supportive families do not need to be in school. Many are better off at home either with their parents or a qualified child-care provider. If you are able to be at home with your two-year-old, don't worry that he or she may be missing out on something by not being in school. Try to relax and let yourself enjoy being with your children and watching them grow. Talk to your children about the things you see and do together. Read to them. Be available to encourage their desire to explore and to help them make sense of their world. You will be giving your children all the stimulation they need. Remember that sending a child to school at two is often a response to the social and economic needs of parents rather than to the academic or developmental needs of the child.

There are, however, a few children this age who seem really hungry for new experiences. These are the children who may benefit from the opportunity to go to early childhood school. Early childhood educators often refer to the special programs they have developed for two-year-olds as "toddler programs." If you decide to send your two-year-old to school it is important that you choose one where the atmosphere is as much like home as possible—nurturing and secure, as well as stimulating. It should be a school where children are not expected to share or made to participate in group activities before they are ready. Lydia Spinelli, director of the Brick Church School in New York City, advises parents, "A toddler program mustn't be a watered-down version of a three-year-old program. . . . It is particularly important for teachers to adapt to a toddler rather than to expect him or her to adapt to them."

The environment in an early childhood school should be interesting and stimulating. It should not, however, be overly noisy or confusing with too many activities all going on at the same time. Beware of schools that promise to teach your toddler how to read and use flash cards and other inappropriate materials. Some studies have indicated that pressuring a child to learn skills such as reading before the child is ready can backfire and cause problems later on in school. Jane Healy, a learning specialist formerly on the faculty at Cleveland State University, reports in her recent book, *Your Child's Growing Mind,* "It is possible to force skills by intensive instruction, but this may cause the child to use immature, inappropriate neural networks and distort the natural growth process."[3] (See chapters 1 and 2 for more information on selecting an appropriate school for your child.)

While child development experts agree that for most children participation in a toddler program will probably make little difference in their long-term physical, emotional, and cognitive development, there are a few children for whom it could make a positive difference:

1. Children without ready access to other children or to an outdoor play space;
2. Children from two-career families who might otherwise spend the day at home alone with a housekeeper who may have little training in child development;
3. Children living in homes where English is not the primary language;
4. Children from economically or socially disadvantaged backgrounds;
5. Children from difficult home situations;
6. Children with special needs.

On the other hand, there are children who would benefit more from spending another year at home or in an informal play group run by their mothers, fathers, or a familiar caregiver. These are children who need gradually to get used to being with other children and adults. Some of these children are so closely bonded to their mothers and fathers that they consistently refuse to leave their laps in a new environment despite the enticements of friendly, reassuring adults and interesting toys. Other children are so scattered that they run constantly from one toy to the next without being able to concentrate even briefly on anything, often seeming to be unaware of the adults and children around them.

Andrew J. was one of the children I have seen for whom the transition from home to early childhood school was too abrupt. Andrew was the only child of older parents with well-established careers. He was a normal, bright, but somewhat reserved baby. His mother, a psychologist, gave up her practice to be at home with Andrew. The two were very close and spent much time alone together while his father was away on business trips. Just before Andrew's second birthday, his mother decided to return to her practice on a full-time basis. She was concerned about the lack of playmates in their neighborhood. She was also unable to find a suitable caregiver to provide the stimulation that she felt was important and that Andrew had grown accustomed to. Her solution was to enroll Andrew in a toddler program five mornings a week.

Although Andrew had had no trouble relating to the other children he occasionally saw on a one-to-one basis at home, he was overwhelmed at being in unfamiliar surroundings away from his mother, amidst a group of children he had never seen before. He reacted by becoming irritable and hard to please at home. At school he was fretful and disorganized. He clung to the teacher and demanded her undivided attention. He couldn't share with the other children and didn't know how to play with them. Fortunately, the school and his teacher were understanding and flexible. The teacher gave him individualized projects and ar-ranged special play areas for him near her so he wouldn't be bothered by the other children. His mother changed her sched-ule so she could spend more time with Andrew after school. Slowly Andrew began to adjust to being in school and demanded less individual attention, but he continued to have trouble relating to other children and being part of a group. He is now five and is just beginning to relate to children in group situations. He likes children but still isn't sure how to play with them. For Andrew, separation from home and mother came too soon and too abruptly. He would have benefited from more exposure to other children in smaller doses in the familiar surroundings of home or in a parents' play group several hours a week before attending the toddler program.

Often it is the parent, not the child, who is really in need of a toddler program. And again there is nothing wrong with this. Parents should not feel guilty because they recognize that they need time off from their two-year-olds. As Louise Bates Ames and J. A. Chase said in their book *Don't Push Your Preschooler,* "It takes a super strong parent to keep up with one of these often adorable creatures twenty-four hours a day. . . . It is important to recognize your own personal tolerances, your limits of energy."[4] Parents need time to themselves to replenish their energy and to continue to grow as people. They also require time to pursue careers, and time to spend with other adults. Parents should be able to do this without worrying about how their children are being cared for in their absence. Many mothers and fathers find themselves living far away from the homes of their childhood, far from friends and relatives. Isolated in a strange city, they often need the support of being part of a community of other parents with young children. A toddler program in an early childhood school can offer this sense of support.

•• Sending Your Child to School at Three

Three-year-olds can walk up and down stairs, make fruit salad in a group, and tell you what they do and don't like. Three-year-olds can talk with other children rather than just at them. Many three-year-olds are also able to play with another child. They can express their wants and opinions verbally, and some have a vocabulary of over one thousand words. They love to be read to, and they love to ask questions. They can feed themselves and control their bladder and bowel. Their balance is good, and many can ride tricycles. They can also dress and undress themselves and even unbutton buttons. According to researchers at the Gesell Institute, three is an "age of delightful conformity, happy sharing, comfortable interpersonal relationships."[5] At three and a half, researchers again find many children in a state of disequilibrium. Many seem insecure and anxious. They may twitch and stutter, bite their nails, and suck their thumbs. Often there are daily battles over routines such as baths and bedtime. Many three-year-olds are at their worst around their parents and may project a much more positive image to their teachers or child-care givers. For both parents and children, this can be a good age to get out of the house. Early childhood teachers can also be a good source of support and advice for parents trying to cope with difficult behavior at home.

Three is the age many early childhood schools begin. Most three-year-olds are ready for a warm, nurturing, child-centered school. As we discussed in chapter 1, the teachers should be trained in child development and early childhood education. Schools should have plenty of interesting age-appropriate materials: blocks, paints, clay, sand and water tables, and dress-up clothes. There should also be ample outdoor space for running and climbing. Three-year-olds are curious about other children and adults, and they are ready to begin to have a sense of the classroom as a community. Most three-year-olds are able to manage physically, socially, and verbally at school. They can communicate their likes and dislikes. They can help make corn muffins or work on a collage with other children. They can follow rules, explore new materials, and begin to make friends and do things with other children in a group. Most children this age are ready to separate from their mother, father, or other primary caregiver. They are able to trust new adults, and they are secure enough to interact with them.

Readiness Predictors

Certain factors are often predictive of a three-year-old's readiness for a successful adjustment to early childhood school:

1. A sense of confidence and security.
2. Enough independence to begin doing things for themselves.
3. A desire to explore and to have new experiences outside the home.

4. The ability to separate from parents or other primary care-giver.
5. Sufficient verbal skills to communicate with other children and adults.
6. A beginning ability to relate to other children, to share, to take turns, and to be part of a group.
7. The ability to stay focused, and to sustain an activity briefly—not just to run around touching everything.
8. Physical development within a normal range for the child's chronological age.
9. The ability to deal with the physical demands of the environment—going up and down stairs, using the toilet.
10. The capability to use play materials in self-initiated and directed activities.

•• False Predictors

Parents sometimes focus on abilities and skills that actually have little bearing on readiness for early childhood school. To be ready for early childhood school, children do not have to know their shapes and colors, nor do they need to have the fine motor control to copy letters and shapes. On the other hand, your observation that your child seems precocious or likes to play with older children does not necessarily signal your child is ready.

Gretchen Lengyel, director of The Madison Playgroup and former president of the Parents League in New York City, feels that "most three-year-olds are ready to go to school in the same way they are ready to go to the zoo—because they have the abilities to enjoy and benefit from both experiences."

The teachers and other educators I have spoken with agreed that the only children who should definitely not go to early childhood school at three are those who are (1) very scattered and unfocused, (2) are neurologically unable to control themselves, (3) have severe speech problems, or (4) come from seriously troubled homes. These children may need to be in a therapeutic setting where teachers have the special training and resources to help them. Parents should discuss appropriate local programs with their pediatrician, the head of the pediatric department at their local medical center, or the special education department in their school district. See chapter 2 for more on children with special needs.

•• Sending Your Child to School at Four

Four-year-olds love adventure and excitement. They often seem to be in perpetual motion. They are full of enthusiasm and questions about everything they encounter. They can skip, catch a beanbag, roller-skate, and ride a bicycle with training wheels. Many like to brag and exaggerate their exploits and accomplishments. They enjoy being with other children and can now play together in a group. They enjoy pretend play. They also like to make up rhyming games and tell silly jokes. Many children this age want to bring things to school to share with their friends or invite the friends over to play.

Four-year-olds are definitely ready for early childhood school. They are ready to share and make friends. They are ready to work together in a group with other children. They are ready for new experiences and new challenges. Four-year-olds are ready to experiment with different materials, to explore shapes and colors, to draw and to build, and to make collages. They are ready to learn how things work and to begin to discover and define their world. They seem more self-motivated and their attention span is getting longer. This is not to say that four-year-olds are ready for first grade or kindergarten. It does not mean that they should be sitting at desks filling in blanks in workbooks or memorizing addition and subtraction facts. It does mean that they are ready for the kinds of quality early childhood schools we discussed earlier.

In the past, access to publicly financed early childhood programs was generally limited to children with special needs. Children defined as needy have included children living in poverty, children with non-English-speaking parents, younger brothers and sisters of children with learning disabilities, and children who have been identified as having possible learning problems themselves.

Today, most educators feel that early childhood school is becoming an inalienable right for all our children, and they look forward to the day when funds will be made available to offer all four-year-olds the opportunity to go to early childhood school.

•• Understanding Separation: When Will Your Child Be Ready to Leave You?

When your children start early childhood school, you will wonder and frequently worry about how they will handle separation. Over the years parents have often questioned me about whether their children will be able to separate and, if they do, whether the separation could be harmful. A 1954 British study on maternal deprivation concluded that "lasting separation before age 2 is the only type of separation that can be shown to be deleterious in and of itself."[6] Subsequent research, as well as the personal experience of countless teachers and parents, indicates that short separations of the type involved in early childhood school are not harmful to children and do not have a negative effect on the natural bonds between parents and children.[7]

The late John Bowlby, at the Tavistock Clinic in London, did some of the classical studies on separation. He found that many children experience separation in three stages, though not always in the same order. In the first stage, the child actively protests the separation and does everything possible to prevent it from occurring. Some children do not protest immediately and may take several weeks to show their feelings. In the second stage of separation, children realize the failure of their protests and withdraw in despair, often showing little interest in other people or activities. The third stage consists of either a successful adjustment, in which the child becomes involved with the other children and in the classroom activities, or a lack of adjustment, in which the child becomes emotionally detached and avoids others, sometimes even the parents when they return at the end of the day.[8]

Psychologists have found that as painful as it may seem at the time, separation anxiety can actually serve a useful purpose by bringing the child and the teacher closer and making the teacher more aware of the child's needs. It is also important for parents to remember that, as early childhood development specialist Kathe Jervis points out, "the clinging and crying of very young children are healthy ways of expressing feelings and learning to cope."[9]

The age your children start school is a key factor in whether or not they will have difficulty separating from you. British psychologist Penelope Leach writes in her book *Your Baby and Child*, "There is nothing more devoted than a six month baby who has been allowed to attach himself to his mother—except that same baby three months later! . . . At around eight months he tries to keep you in sight every moment of his waking day; . . . [when this is impossible, the baby] will be uneasy, tearful or even panic-stricken."[10] Some time between the ages of one and a half and two years, psychologists have found, children's growing awareness that they are really separate from their parents gives them an acute sense of their own smallness and vulnerability. Children at this age will often make desperate attempts to regain a sense of unity with their parents. Separation anxiety, characterized by constant demands and by clinging to parents and shadowing their every move, is an expression of a child's need to try to restore the lost sense of closeness and intimacy. Shortly after age two, however, many children begin to feel more comfortable with their sense of themselves as separate from their parents. This is also a time when many children are beginning to develop relationships outside their immediate families.

One of the reasons very young children have trouble separating from their mothers and fathers is that they believe that when their parents leave the room, they are gone forever. By age three, however, most children are able to retain a mental picture of their parents. They can hold onto this picture when their parents are out of sight and know that they will indeed come back. In his recent book *The Woman Who Works, the Parent Who Cares*, Sirgay Sanger, M.D., founder and director of the Early Care Center in New York City, describes ways parents can help their children develop a mental picture. However, the age at which individual children are able to separate easily from their parents can vary dramatically, even between children in the same family. Teachers often find that children with exceptionally close ties to their mothers and fathers, and no real ties to other adults, find it harder to separate.

Some parents worry that separation will be a problem and are delighted to discover that it isn't an issue after all for their children. One father told me this story about his experience with his daughter: "We had a real fear that Amanda wouldn't want to go to school. She wasn't separating well. Every time we went out and left her with a baby-sitter, there would be a scene. But on the first day of school we were there and saw, to our astonishment, that our daughter was making friends with other children. It was a transformation; she really looked forward to going to school after that."

No matter how well you plan and think you have prepared your children, they may suddenly react in a totally uncharacteristic fashion when the moment comes to separate. In my own family, my son was always the one who approached both strangers and new experiences with a tentative wariness and cried in anguish when I left the room. However, to my surprise and delight, on the first day of school James trotted off quite happily with the teacher. My daughter, on the other hand, had always loved everything new and different; from the time she could crawl, she would go off on her own explorations. Everyone said Diana was just like her grandmother who, family legend has it, was always heading for California with her billy goat and wagon. But on the first day of school, my formerly fearless daughter suddenly and unexpectedly clung to me so tightly that it took both teachers to pry her loose. I can still see her outstretched arms and hear her heartrending cries as I left the room with the teacher assuring me that everything would be fine once I was out the door. I slunk out, feeling I had just abandoned my child. Ten minutes later I called from the phone booth on the corner and discovered to my relief that everything was indeed fine and Diana was happily building a castle out of blocks with two new friends.

As parents we are apt to think of separation as a one-time crisis. Once we have successfully weathered it, we tend to believe we will never have to worry about it again. But this is not always the case. Ellen Galinsky finds that children do "not separate once and for all" but rather that "separation is a gradual process of venturing out and returning for reassurance."[11] Separation problems are quite apt to reappear when you think they are a thing of the past. They often resurface after a school vacation, a bout with the flu or chicken pox, or even after a favorite teacher has been out sick. The prospect of going to a new school can also cause difficulties to reappear. Teachers notice that about the time children turn five and start talking about kindergarten, they sometimes show anxiety and need to be reassured that they don't have to leave their present school and all their friends that very day.

Suggestions for Dealing with Separation

1. Help your child become accustomed to being looked after by someone other than you—such as a grandparent, a friend, or a baby-sitter—before starting school.

2. Don't talk about all the exciting things you will be doing while your child is in school, such as taking the dog for a run or going to the playground with a younger sibling.

3. Include your child in planning what he or she will wear on the first day. Discuss whether your child wants to take a favorite toy to school safely tucked away in a backpack.

4. Talk to your child enthusiastically about the friends he or she will see at school and all the exciting new things they will do together. Remind your child of previous visits you made together to the school and discuss some of the things you found especially interesting.

5. Try to leave the house in a good frame of mind. Plan to get up early enough so you won't have to argue with your children about eating faster or letting them put their socks on themselves and so you are not frantically dashing around looking for your briefcase while the car pool is waiting.

6. Say good morning to the teacher and make sure the teacher knows your child has arrived and is helping your child get involved in some interesting activities.

7. Never try to sneak out of the room when your child isn't looking. Always say good-bye. If you don't your child won't trust you next time and consequently will be reluctant to let you out of sight.

8. When you decide it's time to leave, say good-bye and leave quickly. Don't linger for one last kiss and then another. You'll only make things worse.

9. Arrive promptly at pick-up time. Children may feel abandoned if they are still waiting after all their friends have been picked up.

10. Sometimes our children find it easier to separate from one parent than from the other. If this is the case with your child, let that parent be the one to take the child to school.

If your child has trouble separating from both parents, you might consider having a grandparent or a sitter take the child to school for a while.

Separation is easiest when children have experienced trust in their family environment. In building this trust, consistency and support are very important. We also need to try to help our children feel that it is all right to try new things and even to be wrong sometimes, to take chances and to make mistakes. Sometimes our expectations for our children are based on memories of our own childhood experiences and feelings. One mother whose child separated easily recalled that when she started school, she couldn't wait for her mother to leave. She didn't even want her to walk her to school. If parents believe school is going to be an exciting experience and that their children will be safe and happy, there is a very good chance that their children will feel the same way. Finally, try not to overreact if, despite having done all the right things, your child does cry at your departure. Remember, it is very likely your child will be perfectly fine once you are safely on your way.

•• When You Are Ready for Your Child to Be Ready

When you are ready for your child to be ready for school, your child probably will also be ready. A parent's readiness can be more important to a child's successful adjustment to early childhood school than the child's own level of readiness. Teachers in early childhood schools find it is often the parent and not the child who is not ready to separate. Some parents simply are not ready to let go. They still need to feel needed all the time. Some secretly fear that their child will indeed go running off down the hall at school with never a backward glance.

These feelings are very natural and should not be cause for concern. According to Dr. Robert A. Furman, assistant professor of child psychiatry at Case Western Reserve University in Cleveland, the parent feels both anxiety about the child's performance in a new environment and sadness at what appears to be the end of the first phase of childhood. Furman cautions parents that "until a mother has cried with the sadness of missing her child, she will not be able to help him [her] in dealing with any of his [her] feelings associated with missing her."[12]

Some schools hold informal group sessions for parents to help them deal with separation. A number of working parents have told me that they feel the separation experience at school is harder on them than on parents who are at home with their children. As an attorney explained, "All of us who work feel so vulnerable because we're not there with our children. As soon as I left the room I heard my daughter screaming, 'Mommy! Mommy! Mommy!' I was shaking; it was the hardest thing I had ever been through." Some working mothers tell me that they feel the experience of separation can be particularly difficult for parents with high-powered careers who are used to controlling their world. They may tend to see their child going off to school as their losing control for the first time. Even though they are used to leaving their children with baby-sitters, some feel school is different because, as one mother said to me, "We hire the baby-sitters to look after our children and make them feel good. And if things don't work out we can always find someone else. At school we're no longer in control over how our children will be judged or even who will judge them."

If you have such concerns about separating from your children, it would be helpful to talk with parents of slightly older children who have been through the process and can offer reassurance based on experience. At the same time, try to hide your concerns from your children; be careful not to inadvertently communicate your uneasiness either in words, by telling children over and over again how much you are going to miss them, or through body language, by lingering too long over good-byes. If children sense their parents are anxious about a new experience such as going to school, they may also become anxious and carry this anxiety with them.

Many parents do not worry about the short separation from their children that school brings. If you are one of these parents, you should realize that this, too, is a very natural reaction and not feel guilty. Many devoted parents see their children's time in early childhood school as a brief respite from the constant emotional and physical demands of child raising. They see it as an opportunity to begin to get their own careers back on track, a time to think about going back to graduate school, to finish a dissertation or the novel that was started before the baby was born—or even to read the newspaper before the news is two weeks old. One mother told me that when her fourth child started school, a friend caught her skipping down the road.

•• Compatibility Between Parents and School

Perhaps the most important factor of all in the successful adjustment of children to an early childhood school is the children's intuitive sense of a fundamental compatibility between their parents and their school, a sense of shared values and goals, and the knowledge that both parents and school are working together for the children's best interests. As one early childhood educator said, "If adults don't trust the program, the child won't trust it and be able to make friends and take advantage of all that is going on."

•• Conclusion

Most children are ready for early childhood school at three. Some are ready before three. They have the ability to cope successfully with the social, emotional, and intellectual challenges of being part of a group. They can enjoy interacting with other children and adults and with a variety of interesting materials in a new environment outside their home. They are ready for a school where the teachers are trained in early childhood education, where the activities are individualized enough to meet their needs in a stimulating but noncompetitive environment, and where the curriculum is based on the development of the whole child. Most children are ready for early childhood school because their parents have loved them and helped to make their lives comfortable, happy, and secure. As a result, they have the confidence and trust to relish the challenge of new experiences.

Some children will go to early childhood school whose parents have not been able to give them this sense of confidence and security. And some of these children will find the love and trust and confidence at school that other children have found at home. Children will go to early childhood school for a variety of social and economic reasons that have little to do with their competencies or the developmental milestones they have passed. If the school is sufficiently flexible, and the teachers and parents are caring and patient, these children, too, will adjust in time.

The age at which your child should begin an early childhood school is a question that cannot be answered by either parents or educators alone. The answer will not come from standardized tests, questionnaires, or formal studies. It will come from a knowledge of the nature of available early childhood schools and of the needs and nature of your individual child. Going to early childhood school won't make your child a future valedictorian or a Westinghouse finalist. It doesn't guarantee an Ivy League education or the presidency of IBM. But it may give your child a taste for the excitement of learning and the joy of discovery.

Early childhood school should be process-oriented, not product-oriented. And the process is childhood. Our children can be taught many skills: they can learn to count and to recite the alphabet; they can be taught to identify shapes and colors and to read and write their names. But their childhood must not be hurried in the process. As parents and as educators, we need to remember that our children have many years to write their names and to study calculus, but very few to build castles out of blocks or to see dragons in the clouds.

Appendix

•• •• •• ••

•• ORGANIZATIONS AND RESOURCE CENTERS

GENERAL INTEREST
COALITION OF ESSENTIAL SCHOOLS
EDUCATION DEPARTMENT, BOX 1938
BROWN UNIVERSITY
PROVIDENCE, RI 02912

ELEMENTARY SCHOOL CENTER (ESC)
2 EAST 103RD STREET
NEW YORK, NY 10029

ERIC CLEARINGHOUSE ON EARLY CHILDHOOD
    EDUCATION
COLLEGE OF EDUCATION
UNIVERSITY OF ILLINOIS
1310 SOUTH 6TH STREET
CHAMPAIGN, IL 61820

HIGH/SCOPE FOUNDATION
600 NORTH RIVER STREET
YPSILANTI, MI 48197

•• •• •• ••

NATIONAL ASSOCIATION FOR THE EDUCATION OF YOUNG
   CHILDREN
1834 CONNECTICUT AVENUE, NW
WASHINGTON, DC 20009

NATIONAL ASSOCIATION OF CHILD CARE RESOURCE AND
   REFERRAL AGENCIES
ROCHESTER, MN
TEL. (507)287-2020

NATIONAL COMMITTEE FOR CITIZENS IN EDUCATION
   [NCCE]
410 WILDE LAKE VILLAGE GREEN
COLUMBIA, MD 21044

NATIONAL PTA
700 NORTH RUSH STREET
CHICAGO, IL 60611

INTERNATIONAL READING ASSOCIATION
P.O. BOX 8139
800 BARKSDALE ROAD
NEWARK, DE 19714

UNITED STATES DEPARTMENT OF EDUCATION
400 MARYLAND AVENUE SW
WASHINGTON, DC 20202

RELIGIOUS SCHOOLS
FRIENDS COUNCIL ON EDUCATION
KAY EDSTENE, EXECUTIVE DIRECTOR
1507 CHERRY STREET
PHILADELPHIA, PA 19102

JEWISH EDUCATION SERVICE OF NORTH AMERICA
730 BROADWAY
NEW YORK, NY 10003

NATIONAL CATHOLIC EDUCATIONAL ASSOCIATION
1077 30TH STREET NW, SUITE 100
WASHINGTON, DC 20007

NATIONAL ASSOCIATION OF EPISCOPAL SCHOOLS
ANN GORDON, EXECUTIVE DIRECTOR
815 SECOND AVENUE
NEW YORK, NY 10017

UNITED PARENT TEACHERS ASSOCIATION OF JEWISH
  SCHOOLS
426 WEST 58TH STREET
NEW YORK, NY 10019

PRIVATE/INDEPENDENT SCHOOLS
COUNCIL FOR AMERICAN PRIVATE EDUCATION
1625 EYE STREET NW, SUITE 412
WASHINGTON, DC 20006

NATIONAL ASSOCIATION OF INDEPENDENT SCHOOLS
  (NAIS)
18 TREMONT STREET
BOSTON, MA 02108

REGIONAL ASSOCIATIONS
INDEPENDENT SCHOOLS ASSOCIATION OF THE CENTRAL
  STATES
THOMAS REED, PRESIDENT
1400 WEST MAPLE AVENUE
DOWNERS GROVE, IL 60515

INDEPENDENT SCHOOLS ASSOCIATION OF THE
  SOUTHWEST
RICHARD W. EKDAHL, EXECUTIVE DIRECTOR
P.O. BOX 52297
TULSA, OK 74152

PACIFIC NORTHWEST ASSOCIATION OF INDEPENDENT
    SCHOOLS
SR. SANDRA THEUNICK, PRESIDENT
FOREST RIDGE SCHOOL
4800 139TH AVENUE SE
BELLEVUE, WA 98006

SOUTHERN ASSOCIATION OF INDEPENDENT SCHOOLS
JOHN H. TUCKER, JR., PRESIDENT
NORFOLK ACADEMY
1585 WESLEYAN DRIVE
NORFOLK, VA 23502

INDEPENDENT SCHOOLS ASSOCIATION OF NORTHERN
    NEW ENGLAND
RICHARD L. GOLDSMITH, EXECUTIVE SECRETARY
P.O. BOX 265
BRIDGTON, ME 04009

INDEPENDENT SCHOOLS ADMISSIONS ASSOCIATION OF
    GREATER NEW YORK (ISAAGNY)
1010 PARK AVENUE
NEW YORK, NY 10028

PARENTS LEAGUE OF NEW YORK
115 EAST 82ND STREET
NEW YORK, NY 10028

PARENTS COUNCIL OF WASHINGTON, DC
GRACE MULVIHILL, PRESIDENT
7303 RIVER ROAD
BETHESDA, MD 20817

MINORITY RECRUITMENT
A BETTER CHANCE, INC. (ABC)
419 BOYLSTON STREET
BOSTON, MA 02116

Prep for Prep
Gary Simons, Executive Director
163 West 91st Street
New York, NY 10024

Early Steps
Angela Flemister, Executive Director
1047 Amsterdam Avenue
New York, NY 10025

Minority Hotline—(800)343-9138
Randy Carter at NAIS

Independent School Alliance for Minority
   Affairs
Manasa Hekymara
110 South La Brea
Suite 265
Inglewood, CA 90301

Assessment
Educational Records Bureau (ERB)
3 East 80th Street
New York, NY 10021

Educational Records Bureau (ERB)
Bardwell Hall
37 Cameron Street
Wellesley, MA 02181

Educational Testing Service
Princeton, NJ 08542

Special Concerns

American Montessori Society
Bretta Weiss, National Director
150 Fifth Avenue
New York, NY 10011

Association of Waldorf Schools of North America
c/o Anne Charles
17 Hemlock Hill
Great Barrington, MA 01230

Association for Children with Learning
Disabilities (ACLD)
155 Washington Avenue
Albany, NY 12210

Independent Educational Consultants Association
Box 125
Forestdale, MA 02644

American Association for Gifted Children
15 Gramercy Park
New York, NY 10003

Center for the Study and Education of the
Gifted
Box 170
Teachers College, Columbia University
New York, NY 10027

National Association for Gifted Children
4175 Lovell Road, Suite 140
Circle Pines, MN 55014

The Orton Dyslexia Society
724 York Road
Baltimore, MD 21204

Notes

One. The Basic Ingredients of a Good Early Childhood Program or School

1. Ellen Galinsky and Judy David, *The Preschool Years* (New York: Times Books, 1988), 413.

2. Fred M. Hechinger, "Can Dewey Offer Relevant Wisdom on Working with the Whole Child of the 90's?" *The New York Times*, 18 July 1990.

3. Harriet K. Cuffaro, "The Developmental Interaction Approach," in *Education Before Five*, ed. Betty D. Boegehold et al (New York: Bank Street College, 1977), 47.

4. Ellen Ruppel Shell, "Now, Which Kind of Preschool?" *Psychology Today*, December 1989, 56.

5. Amy Stuart Wells, "For Montessori, a Revival and a Return to Roots," *The New York Times*, 27 June 1990, Education section.

6. Ibid.

7. Alison Clarke-Stewart, *Daycare* (Cambridge: Harvard University Press, 1982), 85.

8. "Accreditation Criteria and Procedures." Position Statement of the National Academy of Early Childhood Programs, A Division of the National Association for the Education of Young Children, Washington, D.C., 1984.

9. J.R. Berrueta-Clement et al., *Changed Lives: The Effects of the Perry Preschool Program on Youths through Age 19* (Ypsilanti, MI: High/Scope Press, 1984).

Two. A Parent's Dilemma: What to Look For, How to Choose

1. Nadine Brozan, "Dalton Easing the Toddler Rat Race, Closes Its Nursery," *The New York Times*, 22 May 1989.

2. Ellen Galinsky and Judy David, *The Preschool Years* (New York: Times Books, 1988), 415.

3. "Accreditation Criteria and Procedures." Position Statement of the

National Academy of Early Childhood Programs, a Division of the National Association for the Education of Young Children, Washington, D.C., 1984.

4. Ibid.

5. *Early Childhood Education: What Are the Costs of High Quality Programs?* (Washington, D.C.: U.S. General Accounting Office, GAO/HRD-90-43BR), January 1990.

Three. Getting In: A Parent's Guide to Admissions

1. Julie Hazzard, *Early Childhood Programs: State Efforts 1989* (Denver, CO: Education Commission of the States, 1989).

2. *Harvard Gazette*, 4 Nov. 1988, 5.

Four. Parents and Children: Ready or Not

1. Louise Bates Ames, Clyde Gillespie, and Frances L. Ilg, *The Gesell Institute's Child From One to Six: Evaluating the Behaviour of the Preschool Child* (New York: Harper & Row, 1979), 21.

2. Ibid, 22.

3. Jane M. Healy, *Your Child's Growing Mind: A Parent's Guide to Learning from Birth to Adolescence* (Garden City, NY: Doubleday, 1987), 24.

4. Louise Bates Ames and J. A. Chase, *Don't Push Your Preschooler* (New York: Harper & Row, 1973), 164.

5. Ames, et al, *The Gesell Institute's Child*, 28.

6. Boyd R. McCandless, *Children: Behavior and Development*, 2nd ed. (New York: Holt, Rinehart and Winston, 1967), 159.

7. B. M. Caldwell et al, "Infant Care and Attachment," *American Journal of Orthopsychiatry* 1970: 40, 397–412; J. C. O'Connell, "Children of Working Mothers: What the Research Tells Us," *Young Children: Research in Review* 1983: 38, 63–70; Sandra Scarr, *Mother Care/Other Care* (New York: Warner Books, 1984), 19.

8. John Bowlby, *Attachment and Loss, Vol. II. Separation: Anxiety and Anger* (New York: Basic Books), 1980.

9. Kathe Jervis, ed., "Separation: Strategies for Helping Two to Four Year Olds" (Washington, D.C.: National Association for the Education of Young Children, 1984).

10. Penelope Leach, *Your Baby and Child From Birth to Age Five* (New York: Alfred A. Knopf, 1978), 197.

11. Ellen Galinsky and Judy David, *The Preschool Years* (New York: Times Books, 1988), 383.

12. Robert A. Furman, "Experiences in Nursery School Consultations," *Young Children*, November 1966, 84–95.

Index